D0484086

THE CAREER RESOURCE LIBRARY

Careers
as a

PROFESSIONAL
PHOTOGRAPHER

Greg Roza

The Rosen Publishing Group, Inc.
NEW YORK

Dedicated to Abigail and Autumn Roza

Published in 2001 by The Rosen Publishing Group, Inc.
29 East 21st Street, New York, NY 10010

Cover © Bill Bachmann/Indexstock

Library of Congress Cataloging-in-Publication Data

Roza, Greg.
Careers as a professional photographer / by Greg Roza.
p. cm. — (Career resource library)
Includes index.
ISBN 0-8239-3184-6 (library binding)
1. Photography—Vocational guidance—Juvenile literature.
[1. Photography—Vocational guidance. 2. Vocational guidance.]
I. Title. II. Series.
TR154 .R69 2001
770'.23—dc21

2001000978

Manufactured in the United States of America

Contents

Why Photography?

Every day, important and remarkable events occur all over the world. Blink, and the decisive moment is gone forever, just like the fish that got away. Most often, a second glance is simply not good enough. This is why we need photographers.

Photography is an indispensable profession that permeates every level of modern society: private life, public life, entertainment, news, sports, government, religion, science, advertising, and so on. We have come to rely on photographers to take us where we have never been (from the frozen expanses of the North Pole to the mysterious slopes and crags of a Martian landscape) and to show us events (from the American Civil War to the birth of a solar system) we never could have experienced without them. Thanks to photography and talented photographers, the decisive moment can live on forever in the pages of magazines, books, and newspapers; on television; on the Internet; in our homes and photo albums; and in a myriad of other locations in our lives.

Careers as a Professional Photographer

It is safe to say that there will always be ample opportunity for people who are interested in a career in photography. Photographers are the professionals we depend on to capture images and events we may not have been able to experience as they occurred, or events that we may want to relive time and again. Newspapers and magazines display worldwide happenings, from local high school basketball games and town hall meetings to wars and natural disasters. Advertisements surround us, many of which contain photographic images. Families and friends have photos on their walls and bulletin boards. Educational texts need visual illustrations to facilitate the learning experience. Corporations and businesses use advertisements, commercials, training manuals, pamphlets, and billboards to sell their services and products. The government and military need photographers for a diverse number of reasons, from criminal investigation to mapmaking. Artistic photographers have carved a significant niche for themselves in galleries, museums, and private homes.

Photography is a profession with limitless outlets and possibilities. If you think that you might like a career that requires special technical knowledge as well as a strong sense of creativity, then photography might be the one for you. Read on to discover more about the vast, intriguing world of professional photography.

Cameras, Film, and Equipment

2

The best way to find out if photography is the career for you is to get your hands on a camera and use it. Regardless of your previous experience with photography, practice is the first key to success. Take photos of everything you can, from your little cousin Sally to the city skyline (or country vista) that always catches your eye. If you are interested in a career in photography, it is essential that you familiarize yourself with the actual tools that make photography possible.

How Does a Camera Take a Photograph?

Cameras are boxes containing light-sensitive rolls of plastic, or film. Cameras are made so that light cannot enter them until the photographer wants to take a picture. When the photographer clicks a button, called a shutter release, light enters the camera through the lens, which is a piece of glass that focuses the image being photographed onto the film inside the camera. The shutter release button opens the shutter, which is a door between the lens and the film. Whatever is in front of the camera becomes imprinted on the film; this is called exposing the film. The film is made with special chemicals that capture an image that can be developed, or revealed, at a later time. If any light hits the film after this, the photo will be destroyed.

Light is needed to take a photograph (the word "photography" means "writing with light"). Without sufficient light, the photograph will turn out dark and hazy. A flash is a lightbulb designed to bathe the object being photographed in light when the shutter opens. The light bounces off the subject and enters the camera through the open shutter, and an image is captured on film. Once a picture has been taken, the photographer needs to advance the film so that the camera is ready to take another photograph. Some cameras have a lever or dial to advance the film manually. Some cameras advance the film automatically.

Parts of a Camera

Although most cameras make photographs in the same way, not all cameras are exactly the same. However, the following basic elements can be found on most cameras.

- **Aperture** An opening between the lens and the shutter that allows light to enter the camera. Some cameras have adjustable apertures that allow more light to enter the camera when needed. Aperture size is measured in f-numbers; the larger the f-number, the smaller the aperture opening.

- **Aperture ring** A dial on some cameras that adjusts the size of the aperture opening. The settings on an aperture ring, called f-stops, correspond to f-number settings.

- **Flash** An artificial light source. Some cameras have built-in flashes. Others have flashes that must be attached to the camera when needed.

- **Focus ring** A dial on some cameras that brings the lens closer to or farther away from the film. This brings the image into focus. Many cameras focus automatically and do not have a focus ring.

- **Lens** A round piece of glass that focuses the light entering the camera when the shutter opens. The lens actually turns the image upside down when it enters the camera, similar to the way the human eye functions.

- **Shutter** When the shutter release button is pressed, the shutter opens for approximately 1/60 of a second. The longer the shutter stays open, the more light is allowed to hit the film.

- **Shutter release** A button that opens the shutter to allow light into the camera. On more advanced cameras, the shutter release button may be used to prepare the flash or to help focus the camera.

- **Shutter speed dial** A dial on some cameras that sets the amount of time the shutter stays open.

- **Viewfinder** A small box at the top of the camera through which the photographer looks to find the object he or she wants to photograph. With cameras that have a focus ring, the viewfinder also helps the photographer to make certain that the photo will be focused.

What Is Film?

The first films used for photography were, in fact, metal and glass plates coated with photographic chemicals. Toward the end of the 1800s, plates gave way to more convenient and durable film bases, particularly celluloid. "Celluloid" is a common term used to describe a thermoplastic called cellulose nitrate (a powerful explosive) and a similar thermoplastic called cellulose acetate. Some film bases are now made of polyester because it is believed to last longer.

Camera film comes in color and in black and white. Although film comes in different sizes, most cameras use 35-mm film; in fact, the common camera is often referred to as a 35-mm camera. Film also comes in different "speeds" (a term that refers to the amount of light that is allowed to hit the film). High-speed film is more sensitive to light than is low-speed film. However, photographs taken with high-speed film can turn out grainy.

How Does Film Work?

Celluloid film bases are coated with light-sensitive chemicals commonly known as silver salts (iodine, silver chloride, or bromide). Silver salts capture a latent (hidden) image when exposed to light, which becomes visible during the developing process. Color film has several layers of colored silver salts. The silver salts are adhered to the film base with the aid of gelatin, which is a natural polymer made from the bones and hides of animals. Together, the silver salts and gelatin form a substance called an emulsion.

Once the silver salts have captured a latent image, the image needs to be developed so that it will be visible. A chemical called a developer changes the chemicals on the film and creates a negative—so named because it displays colors that are the opposite of those actually making up the photograph. On the negative of black-and-white photographs, light objects appear dark and shadows appear light. Then the negative is placed in a solution called a fixer, which prohibits the film from reacting to light any further.

To create a positive image, or a print, a photographer shines a special light through the negative, casting another latent image onto a new piece of photographic paper. Positives can be duplicated from a negative as many times as the photographer wishes. The photographer immerses the positive latent image in a developer to make it visible, the image is fixed, and a photo is born.

Photography Equipment

The equipment you will need will partially depend on what type of photography you want to specialize in. For instance, photographers who take portraits in a studio may want to invest in different styles of backgrounds to be able to offer clients a wider variety of looks: a neutral blend of watercolors, a Christmas scene with a tree and a fireplace, an autumn scene with trees and colorful leaves. Event photographers who travel for every assignment will need several types of carrying cases for their cameras, lenses, lights, and film. Specialty photographers, such as underwater photographers, must purchase and maintain equipment specific to their jobs, for example, waterproof cameras and lights, and scuba gear. You may also need flashes, lenses, lights and lighting tints, light reflectors, lighting umbrellas, a remote timer, a tripod (or monopod), tape, a pen knife, a screwdriver, and any other tool that will help you to carry out your job.

Although some photographers are fortunate enough to work for an employer who will purchase some or all of their equipment for them, freelancers almost always have to purchase their own equipment. As you gain experience taking photographs, you will probably come across the most cost-effective means of buying equipment. Some photographers buy wholesale directly from manufacturers. Others develop a frequent-buyer status with stores. (See the For More Information section at the end of this book for more information on where to purchase photography equipment.)

The Darkroom and Darkroom Equipment

A darkroom is an enclosed area that shuts out light in order to avoid overexposing film. A basement is an ideal place to set up a darkroom, especially one that has a sink and running water. Other places might include a closet, a bathroom, or even a large duffel bag or enclosed compartment that you can insert your arms into and work by touch. Some darkrooms are equipped with a special light with a red filter, called a safelight, so that photographers can see what they are doing without ruining their hard work.

Other darkroom accessories that you may need include:

- Sink with running water
- Counter space
- Shelves
- Developing chemicals
- Photographic paper
- Deep trays to hold developing chemicals
- Paper trimmers or scissors
- Clothesline from which to hang wet photos
- Timer
- Funnel
- Permanent marker
- Small flashlight
- Tongs

Although developing photos is enjoyable for serious photographers, it is also a complicated, potentially dangerous process. The chemicals (sodium sulfate, silver nitrate, lead nitrate, ammonium, and various acids) can cause health problems and injuries. Mixing the developer and the fixer in a typical darkroom procedure creates sulfur dioxide, a poisonous gas, so darkrooms must be well ventilated. It is a good idea to read a few books about darkrooms and developing film before giving it a try (see the For Further Reading section at the back of this book). The best thing to do is to find someone who can show you the process from beginning to end. Keep in mind that it will take considerable time and money to set up a darkroom.

Motion Picture Cameras

Except for a few essential differences, motion picture cameras work much the same way that regular cameras do. Every second, a motion picture camera takes multiple photos on a long roll of film. As the shutter opens, the film is exposed to light and a latent image is recorded. Then, the shutter closes and the film is automatically advanced to set up the next exposure. It may seem that this process moves without stopping the film, but the film needs to stop for a fraction of a second to allow light to hit its surface and capture a clear image. This happens about twenty-four times a second and is called intermittent motion. Sound is recorded in the form of electrical currents directly on a section of the film so that it corresponds perfectly with the action. After the film is developed and run through a projector, the series of photographs and sounds create a moving picture, or movie.

Electronic Imaging

Video cameras and camcorders are simpler versions of motion picture cameras. Video cameras create an electronic current that is recorded to videotape.

Videotape does not need to be developed, and it can be erased or taped over multiple times. When viewed later with a videocassette recorder (VCR), the electronic currents on videotape are transformed back into visual and audio information that can be enjoyed on a television screen. These inventions and their technology are referred to as electronic imaging. A camcorder is a video camera and a VCR in one. Camcorders use smaller types of videotape (8 mm), which can be played back on the camcorder itself. These units can be plugged into a television, and their tapes can then be viewed on the television screen.

Digital cameras are similar to regular cameras. They have a lens, a viewfinder, a flash, and a way to focus the image before snapping the photo. However, digital cameras use a computer chip that converts light to an electronic file that can be saved on a removable disk. This disk allows a photographer to transport an image from the digital camera to a computer. The images can be sent to other people via e-mail, used as part of a Web site, saved to a floppy disk or CD, or printed out on photographic paper. Most digital cameras come with a view screen that displays the images that are stored in memory. With this function, photographers can erase poor shots.

Once a digital image is saved to a computer, it can be altered and touched up with photo-editing software. The photographer can clean up red eyes or fix a poorly centered shot.

Starting a Career in Photography

3

The most valuable advice one can offer an aspiring photographer is to go out and take photographs of things that interest you: animals, natural settings, family members, sporting events, weather developments— anything at all. It is vital that you use your equipment, become comfortable with it, and master it. The more photos you take, the better you will become.

As you amass photographs, scrutinize your work. What do you like about your photos? What could be improved? Which are your most effective shots and why? Which are your least effective shots and why? What happens when you experiment with the depth of field, with light sources, with shutter speed? Analyzing your work is sure to help you improve. It may also help to ask a friend or family member what he or she thinks about your photos. A second opinion is always helpful when perfecting your talent.

Education and Experience

There are countless sources for individuals who want to teach themselves: books, videos, periodicals, Web sites, camera stores, and friends or family members who are also interested in photography. Regardless of how much you teach yourself, there will come a time when a formal—or not so formal—education will become necessary.

High School

Many high schools offer classes in photography. If your school does not have an established photography class, there are still other options at the high school level. Some schools hire students to take photographs for school newspapers and yearbooks. Likewise, you may have the opportunity to gain experience by working as a photographer for the Boy Scouts or Girl Scouts or any similar youth organization.

Mentors

Many beginning photographers learn how to take and develop photographs from an art teacher, a parent, an older brother or sister, an aunt or uncle, or a friend of the family. A mentor provides budding photographers with the opportunity to work one-on-one with a knowledgeable individual who has already made the mistakes, discovered the secrets, and taken the "perfect" shot. An individual learning from a mentor rarely has to share his or her time with other students, which may be another advantage of having an experienced coach. However, one should not underestimate the value of working with other photography students, since you will no doubt learn from the questions that others may ask along the way.

Continuing Education

Many community colleges, universities, high schools, and local clubs offer continuing education classes on a wide range of topics, including photography. These classes are usually more affordable than college classes. Continuing education classes usually meet a few nights a week, making them convenient for those with nine-to-five jobs. Check with local high schools and colleges for continuing education schedules.

Associations, Workshops, and Competitions

Most serious photographers become members of one or more photography associations. Although most, if not all, have members' fees, they are valuable resources. Members of photography associations often receive benefits nonmembers miss out on, including seminars, trade magazines (which feature job openings, workshops, and contests), conventions, product discounts, travel discounts, car rental reimbursement, and sometimes admission to classes taught by industry professionals. The benefits are well worth the dues required by these associations.

Workshops are another option. For a fee (large or small depending on the caliber of the instructor), aspiring photographers can gain insight from experienced professionals. Competitions are a great way to gain experience and recognition as an accomplished photographer. You might enter a photography contest established by your school or your local newspaper. Most contests are sponsored by magazines, newsletters, and professional photography associations. (For more information about associations, workshops, and competitions, refer to the For More Information section at the end of this book.)

Is College a Must?

Not necessarily. Some photography positions—especially those related to the sciences—involve highly specialized knowledge. Photographers hoping to get ahead in these areas may need to have a college degree in a related science (such as anatomy, astronomy, or biology). Photography teachers are expected to eventually attain a master's degree; those interested in teaching in a university need a master's degree or a Ph.D.

However, there are many other photography careers that won't always require a college degree. Many industrial photographers benefit from a degree, but it isn't necessary. The same goes for photojournalism. Good portrait photographers often learn their craft by practicing. Although photographers don't always need college experience on their résumés to land a job, it certainly is an asset for young photographers searching for their first employment opportunity. Depending on the college you choose to attend, you may have a long list of specialty areas to choose from, including forensics photography, fashion photography, editorial photography, commercial photography, science or medical photography, industrial photography, and many related fields, such as animation, darkroom management, and airbrushing.

Colleges with photography programs can provide you with the opportunity to learn from experienced faculty, some of whom you may develop a close working relationship with. In addition, you will have the opportunity to work with other students who are interested in pursuing a career in photography. You may be able to join a college association devoted to student photography. And, as in high school, most colleges offer their students hands-on opportunities taking photographs for the school newspaper, posters, school newsletters, brochures, and so on. You may even get paid for these jobs.

A college education may also lead to an internship with a newspaper, publisher, manufacturer, portrait studio, or other business. You might end up cleaning the darkroom after hours or making sure that the coffee machine in the waiting room is full. Then again, you might join an accomplished photographer on a field assignment. Regardless of the tasks—and despite the lack of pay—an internship is a great way to break into the world of professional photography.

An alternative to a four-year program is a two-year program at a community college or a trade school. This option has its benefits, too. First of all, the price may be more affordable than a four-year college or university. (However, there are many scholarships available for photography students.) Secondly, while the class load at a four-year college or university will entail a wide range of courses—including some outside of the photography curriculum—the program at a community college or trade school will be more narrowly focused on photography.

It should also be mentioned that nonphotography college courses can aid an aspiring photographer in establishing his or her future career. For example, while on location in Spain, it would make a photojournalist's or travel photographer's job much easier if he or she could converse freely with Spanish-speaking contacts, rather than relying on a translator or an English-to-Spanish dictionary. Being multilingual will also give you an edge when pursuing freelance positions in foreign countries. (For more information on travel photography, refer to chapter 10.)

Although the career you choose may depend more on your level of expertise than on your level of formal education, it is the author's opinion that four years of college can help high school graduates in many ways. One of those ways is by providing a wealth of guidance and experience through contact with trained individuals. College is not the perfect option for everyone, but it certainly is an option that is bound to give you an advantage over another photographer who may not have had the benefit of a college degree.

The Portfolio

A portfolio is a collection of your finest work that you use to show prospective employers your photography skills. Your portfolio should be neat, well organized, and appealing to the eye. Each photo should be well trimmed and neatly mounted. The portfolio case itself may also say a lot about the photographer. This does not mean that you need to spend a lot of money on it. Some photographers find used cases that are still in good condition (check out a few online auction sites for used portfolio cases, such as eBay and Yahoo! Auctions). Another option is to make your own portfolio case. The quality of the portfolio as a whole should be considered before presenting it to a potential employer.

Your portfolio should be geared toward the type of job you are most interested in. For example, if you would like to have a job in portraiture, your portfolio should contain shots of different types of people in varying environments. On the other hand, if you are looking for a job in photojournalism, your portfolio should be a collection of news "happenings": an election celebration, a house fire, a new elephant arriving at a zoo, or the opening of a new stadium. Some photographers develop portfolios with color photographs, while others concentrate primarily on black-and-white images. It may be a good idea to tailor your portfolio to what the interviewer is looking for; in other words, don't bring a landscape portfolio to an interview for a job as an underwater photographer.

Photographers who would rather not narrow their options to only one area sometimes compile multiple portfolios to ensure that they have the right one for the job. Some photographers have an artistic portfolio, a photojournalist portfolio, and a portfolio of portraits. This may help open up a photographer's horizons when searching for a career in photography. Whether you choose to cover all the bases with multiple portfolios, or whether you choose to focus on a single area of expertise, it is vital for a photographer to take as many photos as he or she can. You may spend a day snapping shots of multiple subjects and have only a single photograph that is worthy of being included in your portfolio when the day is done. This should not be considered an unsuccessful day, since that photograph might be the one that helps you land the job you've always wanted.

The Résumé

A strong résumé goes hand in hand with an effective portfolio. A good résumé should be succinct and to the point, and it should list your most noteworthy academic and professional achievements. There are many helpful guides to writing résumés on the market; look for them at your local bookstore or library. (Also refer to the For Further Reading section at the end of this book.)

On the Job

Landing your first photography job can be an exhilarating experience. Finally, you get to use the skills that you've discovered while taking pictures on your own, attending college and workshops, joining professional associations, and so on. Chances are, however, that you'll be working for a new employer within three to five years, if not sooner. For example, although working at the photography studio of a department store is a great first job experience, few photographers choose to remain there for too long. You may spend much of your time at your new job assisting other photographers who have been snapping photos for much longer than you have. This situation may seem unexciting for young photographers, but this is perhaps the best situation you could ask for—provided that the photographer you are assisting knows what he or she is doing. Wedding photographers often hire inexperienced photographers to assist them. Although you may spend much of your time unpacking supplies, loading film, setting up lights, and holding the photographer's coat, there is no better way to learn the ropes.

Working Nine to Five

Full-time photographers have a wide array of career options, including the publishing industry, newspapers, magazines, law enforcement, the armed forces, the fashion industry, television and movie studios, schools and universities, portrait studios, and department stores. By proving yourself to be a talented, hard-working photographer, most companies will reward your efforts with higher wages, better benefits, more respect for you as a photographer, and promotions. You will gain valuable knowledge about photography, and you will acquire knowledge about the industry that will help you prepare for a long, fulfilling career. Depending on the field in which you decide to work, you may eventually earn as much as $60,000 to $80,000 a year (or even more) as a full-timer. In addition to these advantages, you may also receive medical and dental benefits, retirement benefits, stock options, and expenses for travel, meals, and equipment, not to mention the opportunity to work closely with others who have similar interests.

Freelancers

A freelancer is someone who works for multiple employers, offering his or her talents as needed—for a fee, of course. For the most part, freelancers make their own hours. Often, they also get to travel. As you hone your skills, your schedule will become increasingly busier, but your style, talent, and techniques will improve. Other benefits include greater work variety, multiple positions, being your own boss, and a greater ability to work in the area that truly interests you. Depending on how creative you are, you may develop your own niche in the world of photography. The more ambitious you are, and the more jobs you work, the more you will earn. Some photographers sell individual photos and can make anywhere from $10 to $2,000 or $3,000 a photo, depending on their experience, expertise, and reputation. Other photographers are hired to develop ongoing projects that may last a week, a month, or longer; these photographers often collect a regular paycheck, like a nine-to-five worker. Many freelance photographers hire agents to help them find work and to help build their names as talented, accomplished professionals. In the end, many full-timers pick up a few freelance positions on the side to further increase their income.

Portrait and Event Photography

4

Do you enjoy being around others? Do you take pleasure in making people laugh and smile? Do you enjoy attending weddings, birthday parties, bar mitzvahs and bas mitzvahs, christenings, and reunions? Are you a "people person"? These are important questions to ask yourself when considering a career in portraiture or event photography.

Portraiture consists of shooting photographs of individuals and families, whether in your own studio, the studio of another photographer, a department store photography center, or in the homes, businesses, or schools of your subjects. An event photographer must be prepared to travel wherever the event is taking place: in a church or temple, a banquet hall, a backyard, a park, an office building, a family's living room, or in another city or country. Approximately half of all professional photographers are portrait photographers or event photographers. It is a wonderful career option for people interested in pursuing a stimulating and potentially lucrative profession.

Portrait Photography

As a portrait photographer, your schedule and work location will depend on the career you decide to pursue, since many (if not most) portraiture jobs take place in an established studio. A good portrait looks natural and is appealing to the eye. For family members, portraits are irreplaceable artifacts. Although portrait photographers may make their art look easy, don't be fooled. There are many elements involved in producing a good portrait. For example, it is vital to work in a controllable environment or one where you don't have to worry about inclement weather, people and/or animals, and other distractions. It is easier to have the subject come to your studio, where you have everything ready to go: cameras, lights, computers, background scenes and props, processing equipment, darkrooms, waiting rooms, refreshments, and samples of your work. To do a job on the road, you will need to bring some equipment with you and then return to a central location to develop and process the photographs. Some portrait photographers actually do work this way, despite the difficulties inherent in the work. Often, the pay makes up for the hassle of transporting yourself and your equipment from job to job.

Some photographers work for other photographers' studios. Here, you may have to start from the bottom, helping out where and when you are needed, which could include keeping records, collecting money from customers, or sweeping up the studio at the end of the day. Although these tasks may sound boring, a ground-level job can quickly lead to a photography position once you have learned the ropes.

Similar to working for a private portrait studio, you may decide to work for a studio in a department store. These photography jobs are perfect for photographers who need experience. You will learn about proper equipment, and you will most likely have several experienced photographers working above you. You will also learn how to please the customer, which is not always an easy task. Convincing a screaming five-year-old to smile can certainly be a challenge; convincing five screaming children in one day can be exhausting. Regardless, these are the types of experiences that will help you to improve as a portrait photographer.

Some photographers have their own studios. There is a lot to consider when thinking about starting your own business. In addition to dealing with clients and taking photographs, you will need to buy or rent a space in which to house your studio; purchase equipment; advertise in the newspaper, online, or on television; pay the bills; and make important contacts. Owning a portraiture studio is a great career but one that requires considerable planning. Those who succeed usually have full schedules day after day. You might want to consider this option after gaining experience working for another studio.

High School Portrait Photographers

At least once a year, portrait photographers go to high schools and elementary schools to take photographs of students, classes, educators and other staff members, sports teams, school clubs, bands, and school functions. These photographs are needed for yearbooks, graduation photos, and other printed materials the school may publish. School portraits are usually available to students and their families for a fee. Most often, school photographers set up a temporary studio in a gymnasium or auditorium for as long as it takes to snap pictures of everyone in the school. Frequently, the photographer must set up a second session for retakes and for students who were absent. Some schools have their own photographer on-site for the entire year, and others hire a photographer every year, usually the same one (which allows an enthusiastic portrait photographer to set up a multiyear contract with one or more schools). Although this may seem like a lot of hard work (and it is), school portrait photographers can earn at least $15,000 a year, and perhaps more than $100,000 a year, depending on the number of schools they work with.

Glamour Portraits

Another form of portraiture that has become popular in recent years is glamour photography. Sometimes, aspiring models and actors need headshots so that they may shop themselves around to film production companies, agents, and directors. Some people simply want an alluring or elegant photo of themselves. Successful glamour photographers use many techniques to relax their subjects and bring out their best features. These techniques may include using different lenses, proper lighting, knowledge of makeup and clothing, and a good sense of humor.

Pet Portraits

Some photographers specialize strictly in pet portraiture. Pets can be unpredictable, and sometimes they can be dangerous. You must know which animals to coddle, which ones to be stern with, and which ones to keep your hands away from altogether. You may have an established studio where clients bring their pets to be photographed. Or you may take your equipment to the homes of your clients, which is sometimes easier than having them come to you. Many pets are more comfortable in familiar surroundings. As a pet photographer, you may also want to invest in an array of props: balls and toys, treats, catnip, backgrounds, platforms, and colorful objects to grab the animal's attention. Since pet photography can be an unpredictable activity, it is wise to be prepared and to get the photo shoot done as quickly as possible.

Event Photography

Event photography is quite different than portraiture, although the two share common aspects. Event photography is a popular career choice for studio photographers and freelancers alike. Those interested in this career should enjoy being around people and going to family gatherings, such as weddings, birthdays, graduations, bar mitzvahs and bas mitzvahs, christenings, baptisms, reunions, and other celebrations and ceremonies. Event photographers must travel to photograph events 99 percent of the time, and this manner of working becomes second nature to them.

It is a good idea to gain experience in event photography by working with someone who has done this type of thing before. Unlike portraiture, event photographers often have only one chance to get the perfect shot. During a wedding, for example, a photographer will have very little time to snap a good shot of the exchange of rings, even less time to capture the kiss. Timing is an important part of being an event photographer. Not only must you be on time for assignments, but you must be able to foresee the perfect moment to take each photo: when the bride throws her bouquet, when the student receives his or her diploma, when the guest of honor sheds a tear. Mess up these shots and you will probably have to deal with upset family members (not to mention that you stand a chance of not getting paid for all of your hard work).

Proper handling and transportation of the appropriate equipment is a vital part of event photography. Family celebrations are scheduled for a specific time, and if you forget to bring your lights, or a lens, or extra film, or the camera itself, you may cause a family to postpone the festivities in order to wait for you to get your gear prepared. You won't secure repeat customers this way. Many event photographers create a supplies checklist to refer to before each assignment.

You won't be able to make your own hours as an event photographer; working late nights and weekends will be a necessity. Your clients will set your hours for you. Bending over backward for the client, however, is certain to result in a growing list of valuable referrals. Some event photographers—full-time as well as freelance—don't even bother with advertising, since word of mouth is extremely effective in this business. However, event photographers should not underestimate the power of effective advertising. In addition to newspapers, trade magazines, and the yellow pages, event photographers may want to create a Web site to advertise their business.

Most event photographers work with video cameras. Many families want special occasions to be captured on film so that the events can be viewed again. As with regular photography, there are just as many, if not more, supplies to consider when filming a special event, including cameras, film, lights, and microphones.

Wedding Photographers

Weddings are by far the most common events for photographers to record. In fact, many event photographers specialize in wedding photography. Some wedding photographers expand their businesses to include other wedding necessities: dress shops, tuxedo shops, wedding supplies, and/or flowers. There are also several magazines on the market dedicated solely to weddings and everything that goes with them. These publications need photos of weddings, receptions, dresses, flower displays, rings, hairstyles, and so on. Wedding photography is a thriving business, and there is always room for another talented, dedicated photographer.

Starting Out: Get Lots of Practice

The first step for anyone interested in a photography career is to get a camera, the basic equipment, and to start taking photographs. Ask your family and friends to pose for you. Study the photographs after they are developed. Which look natural? Which look forced or over posed? Ask yourself (as well as your subjects) which photos look the most professional and appealing, and why. Eventually, you will begin to understand how to make your subjects feel at ease as you take the perfect portrait.

The same goes for event photography. Ask your aunt and uncle if you may take photos of your cousin's wedding for practice. Snap shots of your brother's graduation. Record the events of your niece's second birthday party. Once these photos are developed, scrutinize them for quality and decide which are keepers and which aren't. As you improve, the photos in your portfolio will also improve.

Who's the Boss?

Every photographer likes to think that he or she has an original style, but event photography might be the one photography career where pleasing the client is more important than shooting in your own particular style. Sometimes it is necessary to disregard your personal opinion about a particular shot when the client is in charge. In other words, you need to learn when to give in. Most event photographers pride themselves on discovering exactly what their clients want and delivering it as easily and considerately as they can. Deadlines are an important part of portraiture and event photography. You must be punctual and efficient, or your clients will be disappointed. The more dependable you are, the more money you will make.

However, you will probably be hired based on your artistic ability. Ultimately, it is a combination of the two—pleasing the client and creativity—that will secure repeat customers and important referrals.

Earning Potential

Your income as a portrait or event photographer will depend on your specific job, the size of the job, your level of expertise, and your reputation. Some school portrait photographers and glamour photographers earn about $15,000 a year, which makes it a great side job. Photographers who work for department store studios may earn from $25,000 to $30,000 a year. Experienced wedding photographers, event photographers, and videographers may make somewhere between $200 and $3,000 per assignment. Glamour photographers sometimes make up to $3,000 a day!

Freelancers and photographers who own a studio can make $100,000 a year or more depending on the amount of business they are able to drum up, the size of their operation, and the number of employees working for them. The longer you practice your craft and the more clients you get, the more you can charge for each session (anywhere from $25 to hundreds, even thousands, of dollars a session).

Jared

Jared's cousin Melanie got married today, and she had asked him to be the photographer. Even though he wasn't getting paid for his services, Jared had jumped at the chance. The last group photograph was of the groom's family. The younger kids kept chasing each other around the dance floor, and Jared decided to leave them out until everyone else was positioned correctly. He was tired, he was losing his voice, and his six-year-old nephew had spilled grape soda all over his shoes, but he was much too excited to let these inconveniences bother him.

After three years of college, Jared was convinced that he wanted to be a wedding and special event photographer. The research he had done indicated that the money was decent, the hours were acceptable, and the opportunities were limitless. At the moment, he had only the basic equipment needed to launch a career in wedding photography. (He had borrowed a camcorder from his school's media center.) He had to finish school, but there was no reason he couldn't start gaining experience and building a client base before graduation.

Finally, the lengthy photo session was over. After storing his camera equipment and setting up the borrowed camcorder, Jared rushed off to join the line of cheerful friends and relatives at the buffet. As he waited his turn, a man and woman approached him and introduced themselves as the groom's aunt and uncle, Mr. and Mrs. Dyson. They complimented Jared on his efficiency with a camera and his ability to organize shot after shot.

"Where do you get all that energy?" asked Mrs. Dyson.

"Just doing my job," Jared responded as he reached the buffet table.

"We can see that you're hungry, so we'll let you eat." Mrs. Dyson was about to turn away when she added, "You know, my daughter is getting married in May. Would you by any chance want to be the photographer?"

Jared nearly dropped his plate and silverware. "But you haven't even seen my photos yet."

"Bring them by when you get them developed. We'd love to see them."

Jared's head was swimming as he rushed through his meal. His first referral! He didn't even have a portfolio put together yet. That would be his next priority, but first things first. Jared checked his equipment again, picked up the camcorder, straightened his tie, and went off to film happy wedding guests with the knowledge that his next job (his first paid job) might already be in the bag.

Photojournalism and Press Photography

Experienced photojournalists and press photographers are adept at capturing the precise moment when news happens: the winning field goal in the last seconds of a championship football game, the inauguration of a new political figure, or the town's fire department rescuing a kitten from a tree. Photographers are paid to capture these revealing moments to accompany daily news stories.

Nearly every newspaper in the world uses photographs (and the captions that usually come with them) to hook readers. Many readers browse or skip major sections of a newspaper before or after reading their favorite section. Sometimes a photograph—along with headlines and captions—can tell a reader all that he or she needs to know about a news event.

Photojournalism is often referred to as "telling the news with pictures." Photojournalists and press photographers are as important to print publications as are writers and editors. These professionals help create a visually stimulating product. Publications such as *Life* magazine and *Newsweek* depend on vivid and revealing photos to accompany their stories. These publications show us images of events and people that we might not have seen if it weren't for dedicated photojournalists.

On the Job: Danger and All . . .

In most cases, photojournalists and press photographers spend a considerable amount of time in the darkroom. They also work closely with photo editors when selecting the best photographs for each story. Many photojournalists confer with managing editors and graphic artists to create a unified, effective news article. Putting together one issue of a newspaper or magazine is an involved process that requires the input and expertise of a staff of professionals. Suffice it to say that photographers who work for newspapers and magazines may need to put significant time in at the office as well as in the darkroom.

Regardless, the majority of a photojournalist's work occurs outside of the office—snapping photos of numerous assignments. And these assignments often entail a list of daily scheduled events: ceremonies, celebrity appearances, political speeches, parades, sporting events, grand openings, book signings, weddings, funerals, dog shows, and so on. Events like these are usually on the roster weeks and months ahead of time, and assignments are distributed to photographers accordingly. Whether you're working for a daily newspaper, a weekly tabloid, or a monthly magazine, photographers must pay close attention to their deadlines.

On the other hand, news is not always predictable, and newsworthy events cannot always be scheduled ahead of time. Some events require a photographer who is ready to move out with his or her equipment as soon as possible to capture as much of the event as possible. Freelance photographers (sometimes called stringers) also play an important role in this respect; whoever gets there first is bound to get the best shots. Unscheduled photo opportunities may include natural disasters, accidents, criminal activities, and fires.

With full-time positions, the important jobs, such as political speeches and celebrity appearances, are usually assigned to the veteran photographers, and the less exciting jobs, such as the town square dance, are usually assigned to the rookies. Newspapers and magazines like to send their most experienced and trusted employees to take photos of truly consequential events. Those photojournalists who have performed with competence time and again will start to receive the big jobs; the rest have to work their way up. Small-town papers often have a single photographer, and that person might have several other jobs to fulfill in the office, including photo editor, managing editor, darkroom supervisor, and janitor!

Photojournalists are needed to capture the decisive moments of monumental and dangerous events, such as wars, riots, industrial accidents, and other happenings that may have a worldwide impact. Events like these entail both scheduled assignments, such as peace talks and press conferences, as well as unplanned occurrences, not to mention a considerable amount of danger. Why would a photographer place himself or herself in the heart of danger? Often it is for money, fame, adventure, or altruistic reasons—or for a reason that is less easy to articulate, such as personal fulfillment. When asked why he photographed the events of the American Civil War, Matthew Brady responded, "A spirit in my feet said

'Go,' and I went." Like any art form, photography—even the photography of war—can be a calling that is difficult to explain to someone who does not share your enthusiasm for your craft.

Regardless of your experience, a press photographer's career is a busy one filled with countless assignments. In the morning you might be sent to take photos of the opening of a new fast-food restaurant; you might spend the afternoon in the darkroom developing photos; your evening might be spent snapping shots of a four-alarm blaze in a suburban neighborhood. Travel photojournalists who work for publications like *National Geographic* must be willing to travel on occasion, and they may benefit from knowing a second language. Wherever you work as a photojournalist, you will have a busy schedule filled with exciting—and not so exciting—tasks. Those who succeed at photojournalism are usually physically and mentally fit, eager to perform, and not afraid of the danger that often comes with the job.

Getting the Job Done

Photojournalists and press photographers need to be prepared to take newsworthy photographs whenever and wherever they go, whether they are on the clock or off (some might say that good photojournalists are always on the clock). Get into the habit of carrying your camera (with plenty of film) with you when you go to the mall, to school, or even to the post office. Every accomplished press photographer has a story about the "one that got away," so be prepared.

Taking Multiple Shots

It is also important for serious press photographers to snap many photographs for each assignment. Good photojournalists take dozens of photos, sometimes using dozens of rolls of film. It is unwise to take only one or two photos of a newsworthy event. These few photographs may not turn out, and you will be left without one that is suitable to print.

Deadlines

The news business is fast-paced and demanding. By missing a deadline, you are opening the door for another photographer to steal your assignment. As a result, another newspaper or magazine may "get the drop" on the photograph you were sent to capture. Miss enough deadlines (even one might be enough) and you may have to look for another job. Some photojournalists use digital cameras and electronic imaging to help them work quickly. Take care of your equipment, always have enough film on hand, and be ready at all times for an assignment, scheduled or unscheduled. Your career will depend on it.

Earning Potential

Most photojournalists make between $15,000 and $50,000 a year, depending on their experience and the company for which they work. The average pay for a starting position in photojournalism is approximately $22,000 a year. Photo editors can make between $30,000 and $60,000 a year. You may make as much as

$80,000 a year after proving yourself to be a capable, dependable, and creative photographer.

Ling-Wai

While at the airport preparing to board a flight for Los Angeles to see her father, Ling-Wai and a few of her friends watched the airplanes arriving and departing. Suddenly, they noticed that a plane that had been taxiing into position was on fire! Flames leaped out of one of the engines. Without thinking about what she was doing, Ling-Wai reached into her carry-on bag and took out the camera her mother had given to her last month for her eighteenth birthday. Normally, she took photos of friends and of her pets, but this seemed like a great opportunity to break in her new camera. She snapped photo after photo as the plane stopped, emergency vehicles rushed out onto the tarmac, the fire was extinguished, and the passengers and crew were brought safely back into the terminal.

After this exciting and harrowing experience, all flights were postponed until the following day. As they walked toward the airport exit, Ling-Wai and her friends noticed reporters from the city newspaper and television stations interviewing eyewitnesses. A man with a camera dashed past them, nearly knocking Ling-Wai's friend to the ground.

Suddenly, Ling-Wai thought of the photos she had taken. Splitting away from her friends, Ling-Wai ran to a pay phone and called the local newspaper. She asked to speak to the photo editor.

After waiting on hold for ten minutes, Ling-Wai was addressed by a gruff, impatient voice. Ling-Wai nervously explained the event she had just captured on film. The man's demeanor changed immediately.

"Well, miss, we'd love to see those photos as soon as possible. How soon can you get down here?"

Since the rest of her plans were obviously on hold, Ling-Wai and her friends took a fifteen-minute taxi ride downtown to the newspaper's main office. She was greeted by a tall, well-dressed man. He held out his hand and smiled.

"Hi, you must be Ling-Wai. I'm Jim, we talked on the phone." Ling-Wai proudly handed Jim the roll of film, which he promptly gave to a young woman standing nearby; she disappeared behind a closed door as Jim continued to talk to Ling-Wai.

"Can you wait around for a few minutes? We'll check to see if the photos are useable."

An hour later, Jim came back to Ling-Wai with a big smile and a check for her photos.

"This is what we normally pay our stringers for this type of job."

Ling-Wai's eyes grew large as she looked at the check in her hand.

"Just for taking a few photos?" she asked. It wasn't as much as she made working for

McDonald's for a forty-hour week, but it was certainly more than she thought it would be. A few more of these a week and she wouldn't have to work for McDonald's.

"Three of those photos will be on the front page tomorrow morning," Jim responded. "We're always in need of stringers in the area, would you be interested in working for us?"

"Well, what's a stringer?" Ling-Wai asked.

"A photographer we can call with an assignment when our staff is busy. It's freelance work. Are you interested?"

"Sure!" she said as she looked at the check again. Ling-Wai had been at the right place at the right time.

Commercial Photography

6

Look around you. Unless you're living inside a cardboard box, examples of advertisements surround you: magazine covers, album covers, book covers, cereal boxes, food labels, television commercials, newspaper advertisements, and many other consumer products with photographs, illustrations, graphics, and logos. Step outside and you're certain to see billboards, advertisements on busses and trucks, store signs, and so on, all with photographs and/or illustrations designed and created by talented photographers.

Advertising is the perfect medium for photographers to display their talent and expertise. This is because commercial photography encompasses limitless areas of interest, from automotive parts and tools to gourmet cat food. Not surprisingly, many professional photographers are drawn to this field because of its many job opportunities, high income potential, and the chance to display their creative abilities.

And Now a Word from Our Sponsors

Many commercial photographers work for established companies, corporations, associations, universities, advertising agencies, retail stores, and government offices. Promotions may depend on an individual's professionalism and artistic ability. Many companies hire teams of photographers for advertising purposes, while others use freelance photographers. Advertising agencies hire teams of photographers, editors, and graphic artists to create effective advertisements for magazines, newspapers, books, television, and other advertising mediums. Advertising agencies may also be hired to create logos, product labels, and television commercials.

Freelance commercial photographers usually have the opportunity to photograph what, where, and when they want. Many freelance photographers sell their work directly to photo stock houses, which allows them to focus on the topics that most interest them. One drawback to being a freelancer is that you may not have the same job security you might have working for an established company. This is a drawback for many freelancers, especially those who work hard to establish themselves as talented, trustworthy photographers (and perhaps open their own studios). Many commercial photographers work nine to five and freelance one or two jobs on the side.

Editorial Photographers

The world of magazine and book publishing always needs artists to supply photos covering a boundless range of topics. Magazines hire photographers (often freelancers) to fulfill numerous responsibilities, ranging from product advertisements to cover photos. Some photographers are hired to take photos that accompany the text of interviews, short stories, and articles. Other editorial photographers work primarily with stock houses that sell their photographs to multiple publishers. As an editorial photographer, you can expect to find a plethora of venues to practice your craft, including:

- Magazine publishers
- Book publishers
- Newspaper publishers
- Mail-order catalogs
- Company newsletters
- College brochures
- Programs for concerts, plays, fashion shows, and sporting events
- Business pamphlets
- Stock houses
- Postcard and greeting-card companies
- Web sites

Fashion Photographers

The fashion industry offers many opportunities for commercial photographers. Many fashion photographers get the opportunity to travel, earn excellent salaries, and work with well-known subjects. Fashion photographers may work in a studio, at live shows, or in clothing stores. Fashion photography is a diverse career choice, and not all fashion photography jobs entail working with fashion bigwigs. One day you might take photos of a group of children in snowsuits; on the next, you may photograph adults in swimsuits. In addition to photographing big-name models and designers at live shows, fashion photographers are also needed to film and capture images of clothing for:

- Magazines
- Newspapers
- Books
- Catalogs
- Store flyers and displays
- Advertisements
- Television shows and commercials
- Motion pictures
- Documentaries
- Posters
- Billboards

Entertainment Photographers

The entertainment industry is brimming with interesting and exciting projects for commercial photographers: commercials, advertisements, movie trailers, logos, signs, billboards, and many other forms of advertising. The entertainment industry is a potentially lucrative, exciting, yet demanding business to be in. Much like fashion photography, entertainment photographers often get the chance to meet powerful and famous people, travel all over the world, and earn a high income. Areas of the entertainment world that need commercial photographers include:

- Television
- Motion pictures
- Recording industry
- Performance arts and theaters
- Professional sports
- Books
- Fan magazines
- Trade publications
- Computer software

Stock House Photographers

Stock houses are one of the most profitable venues for commercial photographers. A single photograph sold through a stock house will bring the photographer somewhere between 50 and 60 percent of the fee for using the photograph. In addition, many photographs are sold multiple times to any number of companies that frequently need images for a wide range of subjects. Some photographs sell year after year, continually making money for both the stock house and the photographer. The photos that sell the most are usually the ones that fit in any number of situations: hands clapping, a school bus, kittens and puppies, a sunset, a speedboat, a glass of water, a famous statue, children playing, or a crowd at a rock concert.

Store Photographers

Retail stores, department stores, and malls all over the country need photographers to help create important catalogs, flyers, and other advertisements. Some commercial photographers help arrange and maintain special events for department stores, such as Christmas photos with Santa or promotional giveaways and contests. Commercial photographers working in these venues may have a nine-to-five schedule, or they may need to work overtime, weekends, nights, and/or holidays. Most often they work in the stores themselves or in studios creating advertisements. Some may need to travel, depending on the job.

College and University Photographers

Colleges and universities hire commercial photographers to take photos of the campus, buildings and dorm rooms, sporting events, concerts and theatrical productions, and graduation ceremonies. These photos appear in newsletters, newspapers, brochures, pamphlets, commercials, and Web sites. Commercial photographers following this career path often work when and where they are needed.

Government Photographers

Government offices frequently need commercial photographers for various purposes, particularly to promote tourism. These photographers often take photos of local attractions for travel brochures, tourism guides, and Web sites devoted to the local area. As a commercial photographer working for the government, you will go where you are needed to fulfill your assignments, from town hall to the baseball stadium to the beach. (For more information about government photography, see chapter 9.)

Getting the Job Done

While it might prove to be a creative and technical challenge to photograph certain products—say, motor oil—the commercial photographer who has that assignment must conduct himself or herself with first-class professionalism. Commercial photographers must strive to create fresh, interesting advertising, and also to gain the confidence of employers and clients. Attaining this level of proficiency depends on certain criteria.

Specialization

Many commercial photographers specialize in a particular area of expertise (for example, jewelry, breakfast cereal, or mountain bikes). The more you work with a particular product or subject, the more you will know how to photograph it effectively. What type of light should be used for this shoot? Should you use a zoom lens for this shot? How can you make that plastic hamburger look like a juicy, freshly grilled treat? What would go better with this shot: the beige cardigan sweater or the blue jacket? A commercial photographer is a specialist who must know the ins and outs of his or her job. Concentrating on a single area of expertise and heeding the advice of others who are more experienced than you will aid you in perfecting your photography skills.

Deadlines

Most commercial photographers work with many clients every day, and the pressure can sometimes be intense. For example, you may have a photo shoot at 9:00 AM, and the photos may be due to the client by 2:00

PM. Meeting deadlines is vital to building a reputation as a conscientious, capable photographer. Breaking deadlines is certain to build a negative reputation. You must be quick-witted, you must work well under pressure, and you must be able to make last-minute decisions.

Communication

Commercial photographers work closely with the public as well as with other businesspeople, many of whom might have a say in future promotions and raises. As a result, those who hope to advance their careers must develop valuable people skills. Your success depends on how well you can schmooze or impress people with your talent, expertise, and charm. You may need to make a positive impact on clients, other photographers, bosses, assistants, darkroom supervisors, models, actors, chefs, product manufacturers, commercial directors, or art designers. Effective communication skills might be the deciding factor when you are up for an important, career-guiding assignment.

Creativity

The commercial photographer with the most original vision is bound to get the most job offers. Potential employers want a fresh look, a new angle, a powerful image. Your level of artistry may help land a job with a children's book publisher that creates books on a wide range of topics, or, believe it or not, with a branch of the military designing promotional brochures. The more original and creative your photos are, the more attention you will draw to yourself as a talented, valuable employee.

Originality

The way to develop your own style is (what else) to take lots of photographs and to continually work at improving your work. Equally important, however, is the ability to critique the work of other photographers, particularly the successful ones. What makes their work successful, and how can you emulate their success? As you analyze the styles and results of other commercial artists, your own style is certain to become more original and note-worthy, catching the eye of a potentially long-term employer, or several.

Earning Potential

Many commercial photography positions start out between $20,000 and $30,000 a year, but they can easily rise to $40,000 to $50,000 a year, or more. Free-lancers may earn anywhere from $200 to $8,000 a day, depending on their reputation and ability. Stock houses usually sell photographs for somewhere between $50 and $2,000 a slide. A photographer who runs his or her own studio can make between $100,000 to $200,000 a year, especially in the fashion industry.

Rachel

After graduating from high school, Rachel got a job at her uncle's portrait studio. Rachel was learning everything her uncle knew about photography, the hours were perfect for her (allowing her to spend plenty of time garden-ing on the weekends), and the pay wasn't bad.

Rachel eventually worked her way up from stock person to portrait photographer.

Over the last ten years, Rachel has taken beautiful photographs of her most prized plants and flowers. She has amassed hundreds of photos of flowers, fruits, vegetables, leaves, seeds, bugs, gardening tools, even dirt! Rachel's photos filled up five and a half photo albums. When asked by others why she takes so many garden-related photographs, Rachel had no truly decisive answer. Usually she responded by saying, "It's fun."

One day, while reading Horticulture, *a magazine devoted to gardening, Rachel came across a notice for a photography contest. The magazine's publishers were asking for photos of ripe vegetables that had not yet been harvested. Rachel spent the afternoon flipping through her photo albums until she found a photo of the largest, juiciest-looking tomato she had ever grown. She knew it was a good photo, and it met the contest guidelines, so she sent it in.*

Four months later, Rachel found a large envelope from Horticulture *magazine in her mailbox. It was a letter congratulating her for winning second place in the photography contest, and a check for $50! Also enclosed was a free copy of the latest issue of* Horticulture, *which featured her photo along with the other winners.*

Rachel continued to work at her uncle's studio, but her interest in garden photography had intensified. She entered more contests, and she kept winning. In fact, Home and Garden *ran an article about geraniums featuring a whole series of Rachel's best work. The pay she received for that job convinced Rachel that her calling was not portrait photography but garden photography.*

As her name became known within the industry, Rachel was commissioned to work with several magazines. Soon she began to land jobs for mail-order catalogs that specialized in seeds and gardening equipment. Her photographs were also used for packaging and labeling, from seeds and bulbs to shovels and fertilizer. Rachel sold many of her photographs to multiple buyers through stock houses. Rachel was actually making a living doing something that she loved—it was wonderful.

Industrial Photography

7

Simply put, industrial photographers fulfill the photographic needs of an industrial business or corporation. Although one's responsibilities in this position may include capturing photographs of gigantic machinery, noisy power plants, gloomy warehouses, and hectic assembly lines, an industrial photographer may also help with any of the following:

- "House organ" (or in-house newsletter)
- Public relations
- Press releases
- Advertising
- Periodic reports
- Presentations
- Audiovisual responsibilities
- Product packaging
- Employee portraiture
- Company brochures and pamphlets
- Safety manuals

- Training manuals
- Trade show posters

The Wheels of Progress

Industrial photographers spend much of their time snapping photos of nuts and bolts, canned beans, company boardrooms, mining operations, warehouse equipment, and so on. In addition to understanding the technical aspects of photography itself, you may be expected to understand how the company's products work, how they are manufactured, what elements are needed to make them, how they are put together, who typically uses these products, and how they can be repaired if needed. In this way, industrial photographers are often similar to commercial photographers.

Corporations need professional photographers who can create a fresh vision of their workers, products, equipment, work spaces, and anything else related to the business. Much like commercial photographers, industrial photographers have a challenging task ahead of them: to present the company in an innovative, even artistic light. This aspect of industrial photography might create a great deal of pressure for individual photographers, especially those who are relatively new at this profession.

Industrial corporations mainly hire in-house photographers to work from 9:00 AM to 5:00 PM. Most industrial photographers are required to wear professional attire. Some businesses need only a single photographer to fulfill their photographic needs; larger businesses may require darkroom supervisors and assistants, equipment handlers, lighting specialists, and, of course, the photographers themselves. In larger companies, there is often plenty of room to move up, most often to managerial and supervisory positions that entail looking after teams of photographers. There is also a place for freelancers in the world of industrial photography, and this is often the best way to gain experience in this business.

A Full Schedule

Most industrial photography jobs entail a wide range of responsibilities. In the morning you may need to take photos of products for packaging purposes. In the afternoon you may need to photograph employees and work spaces for an employee training manual. In the evening you may be asked to shoot images for the company newsletter. You might be sent into the field to take photos of a new product or piece of equipment: an airplane engine, a tractor wheel, a mining process, a panel for the space shuttle, or the newest children's toy. Some companies have plants or branches in other cities, sometimes in other countries. You may be expected to take a trip to a mine, factory, or warehouse for other locations for a shoot.

On-the-Job Dangers

One must be cautious when working around assembly lines, flammable or explosive materials, heavy machinery, mining equipment, chemicals, farm machinery, and other industry-related items. Most photographers working for a corporation are expected to participate in a safety course; later, you may be asked to take photographs that will appear in a new safety manual for employees.

Who Needs Industrial Photographers?

The positions mentioned in this chapter are related to truly "industrial" jobs: agricultural companies (such as machinery manufacturers or food producers), automobile companies, construction and engineering companies, architectural firms, chemical laboratories, and a wide range of product manufacturers, from housing material to clothing. Industrial photographers, however, may also find employment with less industrial businesses, such as law offices, Fortune 500 companies, computer hardware and software developers, and insurance companies. You may work in the darkened confines of a steel manufacturer, in the hectic offices of a stock exchange, or on the forty-ninth floor of a multimillion-dollar insurance agency.

Branching Out

The work of some industrial photographers is so good that it may appear in or on the cover of trade magazines, on television advertisements, and on important posters and billboards. Some industrial photographers may get to cover sporting events where a new product is being used (for instance, a new and improved bobsled), fashion shows where a new line of clothing is being revealed to the public, or the opening of a recording studio owned by the leading pop star of the day. These individuals may even gain a reputation as accomplished artists.

Getting the Job Done

Employers won't always require a college degree, although it certainly doesn't hurt to have one. Employers are more interested in results, as well as a positive and professional attitude. Before pursuing full-time employment, you may want to consider freelance work to gain business experience and to get a feel for industrial photography. After a number of freelance jobs, it will probably be easier to attain a full-time position as an industrial photographer. Freelance work will also help you to build an impressive portfolio.

Research Your Potential Employer

When applying for a position as an industrial photographer, do some research on the specific area of expertise the employer is looking to fill. If, for example, the employer is a manufacturer of ceramic cookware, spend an afternoon looking up information about ceramics, cookware, and the related market at the library or online. If the company has a catalog, brochure, pamphlet, or other printed material, get your hands on it and study it carefully. What kinds of photographs are used in these sources? Are they typical or innovative? Ask yourself what you could do to improve on the presentation and marketability of the printed material. Strive to impress your interviewers with your established knowledge of their company, as well as the services they provide or the products they manufacture.

The Industrial Photographer's Portfolio

When creating your portfolio, it might help to concentrate on a specific topic, product, or service, regardless of the type of company you are applying to. This will help you to create a more focused portfolio. You might decide to create a product packaging portfolio, snapping photos of foods, clothing, and other products that would look good in an advertisement or on a package. Industrial businesses are often interested in the overall look you can bring to their company and products.

Be Professional

Many companies look for a go-getter, someone who is interested in moving up in the world of big business. Be prepared to "go corporate," which will entail wearing professional attire, being properly groomed, being on time (or a little early) for interviews and appointments, presenting a positive and attentive disposition, and looking your future employer in the eyes when he or she is talking to you. Of course, this is good advice for most job interviews, but it is particularly apropos when pursuing a job as an industrial photographer.

Earning Potential

Most industrial photographers start out earning around $20,000 a year. Someone with a college degree may start out a little higher. If you are able to work your way up to photographic supervisor or team leader, you may make between $40,000 and $50,000 a year.

Public relations and audiovisual photographers may make a little more to start (perhaps $30,000 to $35,000 a year) because the photos they take will be seen in presentations given to employees, clients, executives, and other important individuals. Some industrial photographers actually run their own businesses designed to create audiovisual presentations for corporations; these individuals may earn $100,000 or more a year, depending on the size and status of their clients. Freelancers are paid by the job or by the day. Those hired merely to assist more experienced photographers may make $100 a day. More business-savvy photographers can make around $1,000 a day. After spending enough time as an industrial photographer, it is possible that you may make $3,000 or more a day.

The biggest, most prosperous companies will want to hire the industrial photographers with the most impressive reputations. By establishing yourself as a talented, efficient photographer of products, employees, work spaces, and services, you are certain to make impressive money as a freelance industrial photographer. The very best have been known to make more than $7,000 a day!

Luca

Luca recently graduated from college with a degree in commercial photography. While continuing to work at his family's hardware store, Luca sent his résumé to thirty businesses that were looking for an entry-level photographer. He received a few responses, but none of the prospects looked very exciting. As much as Luca enjoyed working at the hardware store, he desperately wanted to start building a solid foundation for a career in photography.

When Luca was hired as a photographer for National Hardware, Inc., he was somewhat disappointed. He was certain that the experience would be short-lived.

"I'll stay there for as long as it takes to land a commercial photography position

with an advertising agency," he frequently told his parents. His mom and dad stood behind him, confident that he would make it. Luca's father was proud that Luca would be continuing to work in the hardware field; they even carried National Hardware products—particularly saw blades and drill bits.

The first day of work arrived, and Luca reluctantly headed off for his new job. Once there, he met with Cheryl North, the woman who had interviewed him.

"Ready to learn the ropes, Luca?"

"I sure am," he responded, even though he still wasn't certain this was where he wanted to be.

After Luca filled out some necessary paperwork, Cheryl handed him a lab coat, a pair of goggles, and a security pass with his name on it. Cheryl also had a lab coat and goggles, in addition to a camera atop a tripod.

"Today we're going to break you in by having you take photos for our biannual newsletter. This newsletter goes out to employees, board members, stockholders, the owners of the company, clients, and other companies with whom we work during the year. We like to present as much of the company as we can in these newsletters. We're selling more than hardware here. We're selling a corporation."

The word "selling" made Luca's ears perk up. "So, this is going to be like a commercial photo shoot in a way?"

"Not in a way, Luca. It is a commercial photo shoot. That's one of the reasons we hired you.We need to present our company in its most positive light. Think you can handle that?"

"Sure thing!" Luca suddenly felt more enthusiastic about his position.

Luca spent much of the morning meeting with and photographing employees: assembly line workers, welders, hardware designers, even accountants. Everyone was friendly and happy to meet the newest employee. It wasn't long before Luca felt more at ease. Luca also had a chance to see exactly what went on at National Hardware, Inc., and what he saw fascinated him. This was a fresh glimpse of the hardware industry from behind the scenes.

After a whirlwind of a morning, Cheryl complimented Luca on his style, knowledge, and enthusiasm.

"Now, we'll have you take a few shots of the president of the company before lunch. After lunch we're going to switch gears a little. We have a new line of power tools coming out next month, and we need to get some photos for product packaging and advertisement. We'll be shooting in the warehouse, so maybe we'll also take some shots for our newsletter while we're at it. How does that sound?"

"Sounds great," Luca responded. "I can't wait."

Luca decided to stick around National Hardware, Inc., for a while. It was a demanding job, and he often needed to put in overtime, but the pluses were too good to pass up. Not only was he gaining valuable hands-on photography and advertising experience, he was also learning about industrial photography. He also had a generous medical benefit plan, dental plan, 401k plan, and the promise of a raise when his first three months were up. Luca was glad that he had gone to work for National Hardware, Inc.

Scientific and Medical Photography

8

In this modern era, all aspects of science and technology seem to be leaping into the future at a phenomenal rate. Photography is no exception. Thanks to modern photography, oceanographers are able to explore the depths of the oceans and discover new life-forms and geological formations. Astronomers, who have also benefited from the technological advancements, can now photograph distant galaxies, suns, and even planets, which helps us to better understand our place in the universe.

In the medical sciences, our surgery methods are more effective than ever before, in part because of advances in photography. For example, a relatively new procedure called laparoscopic surgery utilizes a miniature video camera on the end of a surgical baton to conduct abdominal surgery. During laparoscopic surgery, surgeons make tiny incisions in the abdominal wall through which they can insert the video camera and their tools, instead of making large, potentially life-threatening incisions. In this case, photography has revolutionized operating techniques, making surgery safer, quicker, and less traumatic to the patient (who might be able to leave the hospital the very same day the procedure takes place).

Photography is used in many areas of modern science and medicine: magnification, astronomical distances, high-speed and slow-motion photography, fiber optics, X rays, aerial mapping, underwater exploration, research, and education, for example. We have cameras that can capture an image of a solar system forming billions of light-years away and cameras that can capture the moment a human cell divides. Scientists have recently developed a camera that is as small as a pill, which can be swallowed by patients in order to aid doctors and surgeons who are conducting delicate operations.

Science and medical professionals and institutions also need photographers to perform public relations work and to help create newsletters, advertisements, brochures, pamphlets, reports, presentations, textbooks, and many other materials. You may work with employees, patients, animals, doctors, equipment, and paperwork all in one day, depending on your position. Science and medical photographers experience a wide range of tasks, from the ordinary to the highly specialized.

Animal, Vegetable, or Mineral?

Individuals interested in pursuing a career as a scientific photographer have a multitude of specialties to choose from. Depending on what your personal interests are, you may end up working with doctors, military personnel, government employees, archaeologists, oceanographers, astronomers, rocket scientists, or biologists. You also have a wide variety of environments to choose from (again depending on your interests or area of expertise), including colleges, hospitals, corporations, manufacturers, factories, laboratories, or museums.

Photographers are needed in every science you can think of, from archaeology to zoology. In addition, each science has an abundance of photography tasks and positions that need to be filled, from researcher to public relations specialist. There is a large array of opportunities for those who are willing to devote their time to becoming a proficient scientific photographer. This chapter will explore a handful of the opportunities available to you.

Aerial Photographers

Aerial photographers photograph animals in their natural habitats, weather patterns and developments, archaeological digs, and many other scientific interests. One of the most common forms of aerial photography is photogrammetry, the science of making maps from aerial photographs. The military and the government both need photographers trained in photogrammetry to create maps and scale drawings of landforms. Pilots trained in photography may have an edge in this career. Other areas of knowledge that may be necessary include computer technology, cartography, and geography. It is possible to get a job in photogrammetry without a college degree, but your chances are much better with a degree in geography, computer science, engineering, or even general science.

Underwater Photographers

Underwater photographers are needed to help conduct research concerning plant and animal life, the fishing industry, tides, underwater topography, oil drilling, and other marine-related interests. Underwater photography involves knowledge of specialized equipment and technology, especially scuba diving and underwater lights and cameras. A degree in biology (or at least a solid understanding of it) may also be beneficial. In fact, a considerable number of employers looking for underwater photographers prefer that candidates are trained in science first and photography second. In addition to being used for record-keeping and investigative purposes, underwater photos may be used in textbooks and wildlife magazines.

Archaeological Photographers

Archaeologists need photographers to document the artifacts unearthed at digs all over the world: bones, pottery, cloth, metal, tools, and other objects. Photographers must take pictures of each and every object that is unearthed, no matter how small. This usually amounts to hundreds of photographs per dig. Photographers are also needed to record the actual dig sites themselves as layer upon layer of earth is revealed. Most archaeological photographers are employed by colleges, universities, and museums.

Biological Photographers

Biological photographers take photographs of a wide range of life-forms and life processes. Biological photographers also help document new biological discoveries or techniques, such as the results of a revolutionary new antibiotic as it works to fight an infection in a human cell. On the other hand, a biological photographer may take

65

standard photos of flowers, trees, animals, and people for high school textbooks. Some biological photographers work with specialized equipment, particularly microscopes. You may need to have a college degree in biology.

Botanical Photographers

Botanical photographers take close-up photographs of plants, seeds, roots, stems, leaves, branches, fruit, flowers, even soil. They must be familiar with zoom lenses and close-up lighting techniques. Botanists study and run tests on the flora of the world, and botanical photographers document every botanical discovery. Although some of their work takes place inside a laboratory, botanical photographers often get the chance to travel all over the world. Botanical photographers also take pictures for textbooks and wildlife magazines. A college education is not necessary to become a botanical photographer, but a knack for gardening and/or a love of the outdoors may be the key to finding success as one.

Getting the Job Done

It is often possible to land a job in the field of scientific photography based on your photography skills alone. Photographers who have specialized knowledge or education in one or more areas other than photography may have an advantage over those who do not. Most scientific photographers have at least a bachelor's degree in general science.

Many scientific photographers begin as lab assistants. This is a great way to learn the ropes from others who already know them. As mentioned several times in this book, learning from a more experienced individual, or mentor, is the most effective way to become the best photographer you can be. In addition, many assistant jobs lead to higher positions if you have the patience and determination to succeed.

Freelancers are frequently needed to help fulfill short-term projects for various scientific foundations. After becoming comfortable with freelance work, you may decide to continue to work as a freelancer, or you may want to take the experience you've amassed and use it to secure a full-time position.

Some scientific photographers work through specialized stock houses and make money selling their photographs to book publishers (often textbook companies), magazine publishers, and others. You may decide to specialize in underwater images, images of bacteria, or images of human anatomy. Again, this is a good way to build a positive reputation and to move into a lucrative full-time job.

Earning Potential

Depending on your education, scientific background, and experience, you may earn anywhere from $20,000 to $30,000 a year as a starting scientific photographer. Freelancers may earn between $20 and $150 an hour, depending on their expertise. Some entry-level positions in this field are based on volunteer work. Scientific photographers working for the government may begin around $20,000 a year, but they can work their way up to $30,000 and $40,000 a year.

Roberto

Roberto had gained most of his photographic experience aboard a battleship in the Gulf of Mexico while he was in the U.S. Navy. In addition to countless activities, Roberto took surveillance photos of Cuban military activity, and he also took the occasional photograph of underwater geological formations for the government. When his stay in the armed services was up, Roberto earned a four-year degree in biology.

After graduation, Roberto was fortunate enough to land a freelance position as an underwater photographer with a team of government oceanographers. Their aim was to study underwater volcanic action in the waters around the Hawaiian Islands and to create a database of plant and animal life found in the vicinity. This type of project had been conducted several times in the past, but because of new technology, diving techniques, and scientific knowledge, government records needed to be updated.

Before the project began, they set up a grid with the help of aerial photographs that would guide them in exploring the waters around the islands. Each day at sunrise, the team met at a high-tech government laboratory aboard a ship, which promptly set sail to a specified location. By 8:00 AM, Roberto and his coworkers were under the water with their special lights and cameras, specimen containers, and scuba gear. Every day, Roberto took countless photographs of exotic plants, fish and other wildlife, coral reefs, geological formations, lava flows, and underwater hot air vents that warmed the waters surrounding Hawaii. The day usually consisted of three to four dives and hundreds of photographs, which were promptly developed in the afternoon by another team on the shore. Roberto and the other divers, scientists, and photographers were usually finished by 3:00 PM, exhausted by the hard work but dazzled by visions of the stunning underwater world.

The job was going to be completed sometime in the next two months. After three years of exploration and research, the team had made several new geological and biological discoveries. It had been a challenging yet fascinating three years, and Roberto was already planning for future underwater photography projects. He had received another job offer from the government, this time off the coast of northern Maine. However, although the money sounded good, the location did not appeal to him. Roberto had also received a job offer with a private company working in the Gulf of Mexico, territory he was very familiar with. The money would be great, the benefits outstanding, and he would be team supervisor.

It was going to be a hard decision to make. After living and working in Hawaii for three years, Roberto had developed several friendships that he was sad to leave behind. Plus, Hawaii was the most beautiful place he had *ever visited, and he was not ready to leave it. With his experience as an underwater photographer, and the natural bounty of subject material in the waters surrounding Hawaii, Roberto knew he could make a living by selling his own photos. He was already supplementing his government salary with his own private photography, selling photos to publications like* National Geographic *and* Ocean Realm *magazines. He had won several contests, and some publishers were actually calling him for photos. He had a great idea for a book of his own, too, and all he needed was a book publisher to back him. Even though he had not yet made up his mind on the issue, Roberto had a feeling that in the end he would eventually set up shop on the beautiful island of Oahu.*

An Apple a Day

Most medical photographers work in hospitals and laboratories. In the morning of a typical day as a medical photographer, you may be required to make slides for a workshop on a surgery technique used by the surgeons at the hospital. In the afternoon, you may need to take pictures of hospital personnel and work spaces for a hospital safety manual. In the evening, you may be asked to document the development of a new medical procedure.

Other assignments may include taking photographs of newborns, intensive care patients, burn victims, autopsies, surgical operations, tissue samples, or microscopic images. In addition, you might be required to take photos for presentations, medical journals, medical schools, textbooks, and even public relations purposes. Regardless of the task, it should also be mentioned that medical photographers will most often be required to photograph a considerable amount of "blood and guts," so be prepared.

Getting the Job Done

As with scientific photography, medical photographers usually need to be trained in a specific field and in the use of specialized equipment. It is not unheard of for doctors, surgeons, and nurses to take on the responsibilities normally delegated to in-house photographers. This is because they are already specialists in the necessary fields and because sometimes the hospital cannot afford to keep a full-time photographer on staff. Depending on its size and budget, a hospital may have an in-house photographer, or it may hire freelancers when needed. This is another case where a college education in biology, chemistry, computer science, or general science will give you an edge on others who are applying for the same position; in many instances, a college education will be a necessity.

Since new developments are constantly occurring in the field of medicine, medical photographers will be expected to ride the wave of innovation. New cameras, developing techniques, computer hardware and software, digital equipment—all of these and more are now being used in the field of medical photography. If you intend to stay in high demand, you must stay educated on the latest equipment and techniques—photographically, technologically, and medically. A good way to do this is to take any courses or workshops offered by the hospital for which you work. Another way is to subscribe to journals and periodicals related to your career and area of expertise.

Earning Potential

The starting salary for medical photographers is similar to that of scientific photographers, between $20,000 and $30,000 a year, sometimes a little higher depending on the institution you work for and your experience.

Renée

For the past seven years, Renée has worked for a large city hospital as a medical photographer. When she first applied for the position, she wasn't certain that it was the right job for her, especially considering the fact that she had originally been trained in medical billing and pharmacology. (Photography had been a favorite hobby of hers since she was fifteen.) When the position appeared in the want ads, she figured that it might be the perfect chance for her to get her foot in the door with a hospital and that she would be able to work her way into medical billing. Things turned out differently, however, and now Renée is the head photographer with a team of six photographers working under her.

At the hospital, every day is different. Several of the newer photographers are still in training, and Renée needs to guide them through various tasks. Today is going to be busy. The hospital recently began implementing a new style of heart bypass surgery that needs to be documented. In addition, it will be preparing a slide show for surgical interns.

Upon arrival at the hospital at 6:00 AM, Renée begins setting up the equipment her team needs for the morning's surgery. This includes three 35-mm cameras, two tripods, twenty rolls of color film, and hospital scrubs for her two assistants and herself. The bypass surgery is slated for 8:10 AM.

The surgery goes smoothly and ends earlier than the surgeons expected. Although Renée began taking photos in the morning, by 11:00 AM her two assistants take over as she supervises. At 1:20 PM when the surgery is over, Renée and the assistants gather their equipment, store it in Renée's office, and go to the cafeteria for a quick lunch. Three more assistants will join them after lunch when they develop the photos, make 35-mm slides, catalog them for future researchers, and finish up the necessary paperwork before heading home around 7:00 PM. The following day they will assemble the photos into a presentation with the help of a surgeon.

Although this project takes up most of her time, Renée also needs to find time to design a brochure for the hospital that includes information about the new bypass procedure. Her team of photographers needs to take photos of the hospital, the operating room, the emergency room, a few of the patient rooms, the nursery, and the hospital staff before noon tomorrow in order for her to keep on schedule. With her talented team of photographers, she has no worries about meeting her deadlines.

Military and Government Photography

9

The United States military and government are virtual microcosms of society (particularly so with the military) and, therefore, offer photographers opportunities similar to those already addressed in previous chapters. Reading chapters four through eight will help you gain a sense of the options available to you in the military and in the government. Adventurous photographers will no doubt discover unique job opportunities, such as aerial photography, fire photography, and surveillance. In addition, photographers who work for the government or the military enjoy superior benefits, ranging from medical coverage to funding for housing, clothing, and food. Although a career in the government or military is not for everyone, if you are a patriotic individual who is interested in serving your country, it might be the perfect place for you to land employment as a photographer.

You're in the Army Now!

The U.S. armed forces—the U.S. Army, Navy, Marines, Air Force, Coast Guard, National Guard, and the Reserves—need many types of photographers, and enlistees who are able to choose from a wide range of specializations. Commercial photographers are needed to help "sell" the armed forces with inspiring photos for recruiter pamphlets, posters, brochures, television commercials, and other forms of public relations. Videographers are needed to create training films, television commercials, and recruitment videos. Industrial photographers are needed to document tests of new equipment, work areas, and other work-related subjects. Military photojournalists are often where the action is, whether they see actual battles or not. The military has its own system of doctors and scientists who see a considerable amount of work as a result of on-the-job injuries, wounds, and routine checkups, as well as scientific developments and experiments. These photographers may also help industrial photographers make working conditions safer for enlistees and officers by capturing photographs of new equipment and processes.

As you can see, nearly every type of photographer is needed in the armed forces, even portrait and special event photographers. However, some photography positions in the military are designed specifically for the world of combat and warfare. Aerial photographers are needed for surveillance and mapping purposes. Surveillance photographers are sometimes needed to secretly capture images of the enemy, their location, and their equipment in times of war. The military also needs trained darkroom staff and equipment specialists.

How does one go about becoming a military photographer? That's easy: enlist. Not every person who tries to get into the armed forces makes it (perhaps because of health issues or family situations), but if you are determined to get in you probably will. Look up your local armed forces recruiter in the yellow pages. You recruiter can answer all of your questions about enlisting and can aid you in exploring the specific career paths available to you.

On-the-Job Training

Aspiring photographers can expect to receive valuable on-the-job training, which guarantees them a wide range of lucrative photography positions in the civilian world. Trained photographers may also decide to attend college upon being discharged from the armed services (the military will usually pay your entire tuition after you serve for a specified amount of time). Even if you know nothing at all about photography, you will be given the chance to become a pro by attending a crash course in photography (anywhere from ten to twenty-four weeks of classroom education). Formal education is just the beginning, however, as you will be expected to gain valuable hands-on training as you serve your country.

The New Recruit's Responsibility

Most photographers don't join the armed services with the intention of obtaining a good photography job. New recruits who enlist must keep in mind that their chief responsibility is to work for and defend the United States. Joining the armed forces is a decision that must not be taken lightly since it will involve hard work, physical endurance, the ability to take orders, specialized knowledge of a wide array of machinery and procedures, dedication to your career and the people with whom you work, and sometimes dangerous situations. Give this decision considerable thought before enlisting; it is a long-term responsibility that will certainly change your life.

Life in the armed services is often demanding, but it is also highly rewarding. Although the pay is not particularly attractive, potential enlistees should keep in mind that the military will provide clothes, shelter, food, medical care, dental care, entertainment outlets, and other needs and wants of daily life. Many enlistees also get the chance to travel all over the world and see people and places they might not have seen had they remained civilians.

Earning Potential

The pay scale for military personnel is not exactly attractive; new recruits currently make about $11,000 a year. Pay, however, is not usually the main reason young people join the armed services. Patriotism and the desire to meet new people, see new places, and raise money for a college education are a few good reasons for joining the military. If the low pay scale still troubles you, keep in mind the benefits mentioned earlier. As already mentioned, the training you receive in the armed services will boost your chances of employment in the civilian world with the potential to make up for the low pay offered by the military.

Nina

Nina had just graduated from high school. Several of her closest friends had already enrolled in art school. Although this seemed like a viable option for her, too, since she loved to draw and sculpt, Nina did not like the thought of going back to school so quickly. It had been a tough four years. Nina had received passing grades in all of her classes—especially her art and music classes—but she really wanted to see the world and experience many of the places she had only read about. The only problem was money. Nina soon realized that she would need to get a job; without money there was no way to travel.

It was Nina's aunt Sharon, a police officer who had received law enforcement training in the U.S. Army, who had given her an idea about what to do in the future.

"I wasn't sure what I wanted to do when I graduated from high school either," Sharon told Nina. "My father suggested the military. He said that there were many careers to choose from in the armed forces. I joined the army when I was eighteen and was stationed in Alaska for two years. I didn't get to see much of the world, but I got the best training I could ask for. And now I'm a police officer."

Nina gave Sharon's advice some thought before going to see an army recruiter in her hometown. Her parents thought it was a good idea but cautioned her to think long and hard about taking such a big step. Joining the armed forces began to sound like the perfect option for Nina. She loved physical activity, she wasn't afraid of hard work, and the government would even pay for her college tuition after a few years of service. When she told the recruiter that one of her interests included art, he informed her that the army was currently looking for photographers to fill several different positions.

"Well," Nina said, "I do have experience with painting and sculpting, but I don't know that much about photography."

"No problem," the recruiter told her. "The army will train you. And when the training is over, you will have several areas of interest to choose from. We need photojournalists and aerial photographers right now, but I'm sure you could train for any number of photography specialties. We're also looking for darkroom technicians, satellite and digital imaging specialists, and camerapersons who can help film training videos for new recruits. Sound interesting?"

Nina had to admit that it sounded very interesting. She had no idea that the military had so much to offer a recent high school graduate. And photography certainly was an enticing prospect. After talking it over with her parents, her aunt Sharon, and her pastor, Nina finally decided that a two-year stay in the army was the right thing to do.

Basic training was hard at first, but after a few weeks, the physical workouts and class-room course load became easier to handle. Nina really began to enjoy herself by the fourth week. She also made several new friends, and they helped each other grow accustomed to the rigors of life in the armed services.

Soon after her basic training was completed, Nina was shipped out to a base in Virginia. There she began her training as a photojournalist for the army. The class work was new and fascinating for her, but it did not last long. Within a few months, Nina was being sent out on location with experienced photographers to cover military news events. For the time being, Nina was just an assistant, and most of her duties included maintaining, transporting, and setting up photographic equipment, but she was learning faster than she originally thought possible. She knew that soon she would be taking photographs for the army and her future would only get brighter.

We, the People

Much like the armed forces, the government needs many of the types of photographers previously mentioned in this book. Photojournalists take newsworthy photos for government publications. Commercial photographers help to create effective brochures, pamphlets, advertise-ments, and newsletters for federal, state, and local govern-ments. Governments are often considered types of businesses, and industrial photographers are able to find positions working for them. Scientific photographers are needed to document natural resources and the problems surrounding them. Medical photographers are needed to archive new medical methods for governmental agencies. Although they share many similarities, working for the federal government and working for state and local governments can be very different.

The Federal Government

Hundreds of federal government jobs are categorized according to series. Each series has a code; for instance, the photography series is tagged with the number GS-1060. Other series that may interest you as a photographer include illustrating (GS-1020), audiovisual production (GS-1070), and photographic technology (GS-1386). The salaries within these series depend on the photographer's "grade," which is determined primarily by education and experience.

Forms and applications are a necessary part of most government jobs, and you are sure to run into a stack of them before you actually land a job. This alone may deter some job seekers, but it is usually those who accomplish this part with patience and accuracy who are rewarded with an interview, and perhaps employment. It should also be mentioned that many government agencies expect to see your résumé before seeing you.

Again, much like photography in the armed forces, there will be a few specialized areas for photographers to consider. Aerial photographers are needed to help develop maps of landscapes as well as maps of oceans and seas. Photogrammetry specialists are also in high demand. (See chapter 8 for more information on photogrammetry.) The federal government also employs a large number of medical photographers. These jobs might be difficult to attain, but once you do land one, it is certain to lead to a stable, long-term position with the federal government.

How Do I Become a Photographer for the Federal Government?

Becoming a full-time photographer for the federal government is not as easy as it is to become a photographer for the military. Even though there are approximately 3,000 photography positions in the federal government, a large majority of these jobs are freelance positions. Full-time positions are difficult to find, especially when you don't have an inside contact. Here are some paths to consider.

- Most full-time photography jobs are a result of knowing and working for a particular person or division for an extended period of time as a freelancer. The more good work you do for a particular branch or person, the more work you are likely to receive from him or her. Referrals are also an important element to consider when pursuing a photography career with the federal government. Get on someone's good side, and that person will be certain to pass your name and number along to others who are in need of a capable photographer.

• Another way to land a job with the government is to fill out the proper applications and submit them to the appropriate agencies. The blue pages in your local telephone directory are reserved for government offices and personnel. You will be able to find information there on where to apply for government jobs and whom to consult. If you're not sure where to start looking, try contacting the Office of Personnel Management, and someone there will be able to give you a greater sense of direction in your search for a government job.

• Another option is to browse one of the many helpful government employment Web sites on the Internet. Some sites have listings of open government positions. Other sites have printable versions of applications and other important documents for people who work for the federal government and for those who want to work there. Still other sites have helpful guides (sometimes free, sometimes for a fee) for applying and attaining government jobs. (Look for government-related Web sites in the For More Information section at the back of this book.)

State and Local Government

Despite the fact that photographers are in high demand, searching for a government photography job at the state or local level may prove to be as tedious and difficult as when searching for one with the federal government. Also, like federal government jobs, most state and local government jobs pay moderately well and offer excellent benefits. The telephone directory and the Internet will probably be your best tools when searching for a government position. City, town, county, and state governments have countless agencies, such as tourism, forestry, transportation, or agriculture, each of which needs the services of experienced photographers. Try checking with these individual agencies for potential openings. You may also want to check with your local employment agency or with a college or university in your local area—all of these places often keep updated lists of government job openings. And, as mentioned earlier, be prepared to fill out a considerable amount of paperwork.

Just as in the federal government, photographers are always needed to accomplish a multitude of tasks and projects at the state and local levels, such as advertisements, training videos, public relations, portraiture, safety manuals, or scientific studies. Three areas of photography specific to local and state government include forensics photography, fire photography, and surveillance photography.

Forensics Photographers

When you hear the term "forensics photography," you probably picture flashing lights, shouting police officers, twisted metal, and blood. This type of scene is in fact a part of forensics photography, but there is a less dramatic side to this area of work. Forensics photography often entails slow, painstaking, yet highly specialized tasks, including high-speed photography, infrared photography, and darkroom procedures. You will probably spend the bulk of your day in a laboratory photographing various pieces of evidence from every possible angle—a shoe, a dog collar, bullets, a pen, a telephone, documents, even autopsies. In addition to working with local and state governments, you may be required to aid federal agencies like the Drug Enforcement Agency, the Federal Bureau of Investigation, and the Secret Service. Landing a forensics photography position usually entails passing a civil service examination, in addition to having effective photography skills and habits.

Fire Photographers

Similar to forensics photography, fire photography involves documenting a wide range of evidence, primarily fire damage and related causes. You may be needed to investigate a fire that was the result of arson. Fire photographers are also needed to capture images of equipment and employees for safety and insurance-related reasons. They may need to snap shots and record video footage of fires as they are happening, requiring them to wear protective gear and to take courses in fire safety and first aid. Photographers may also be expected to capture photos of equipment, firefighters, and vehicles at work. Many fire photographers are former firefighters. As such, they are frequently expected to work a firefighter's schedule, which often includes long hours and extended shifts.

Surveillance Photographers

State and local governments (as well as federal agencies, private investigators, and tabloids) frequently use surveillance photographers. Surveillance photographers use still photography and video to capture people doing things they shouldn't be doing. A local police photographer may be required to capture photos of an individual who is suspected of misappropriating city funds. A private investigator may be hired by an insurance company when it suspects an individual of insurance fraud (like the carpenter who is collecting disability due to a bad back, but who is discovered playing golf when he should be resting at home). On the other hand, surveillance photographers who work for newspapers (particularly tabloids) usually aren't trying to apprehend criminals—their goal is generally to take photos of famous people in private or revealing situations. Surveillance photographers hide in parked cars, in trees, behind two-way mirrors, and in any other location that helps to conceal their appearances from the people they are observing.

Freelancing

Freelance photographers for the federal, state, and local government are able to make a reasonable amount of money. However, as a freelancer, you must be persistent: search for work listings, call the appropriate offices and personnel, and follow up on your contacts. Making contacts and establishing referrals are vital activities if this is the path you intend to take. Few photographers turn their freelance work into a full-time position, but those who do no doubt spent months, even years, building a solid bank of contacts and referrals prior to freelancing on a full-time basis. In short, freelancing might be your best bet when hoping to establish a career as a government photographer, but that doesn't mean that you'll never secure a full-time position. Hard work and persistence are certain to pay off in the end.

Earning Potential

If it is your dream to establish a career that is financially lucrative, not to mention abundantly exciting, a career with the government may not be the profession for you. Most photography positions with the government begin around $18,000 a year. Surveillance and forensics photographers often start between $25,000 and $35,000 a year because they are usually trained police officers. Likewise, a fire photographer's pay scale is similar to the pay scale for firefighters. Most government photographers work their way up to $35,000 a year. It is possible to make more, and the longer you are with a particular agency the more money you will make.

Much like the military, government positions often come with attractive benefits, so attractive that the low pay does not seem so bad in the long run. These benefits include superior retirement plans, paid vacation time, medical and dental insurance, life insurance, and so on. Also, keep in mind that the government is a very secure working environment; the U.S. government will always be in need of talented, experienced photographers to accomplish a multitude of tasks. This means there will always be a job out there for you in the extensive world of government photography.

Ian

Ian had fought fires with the same city fire department for fifteen years. It was exciting and challenging, not to mention fulfilling, to help others in need on a daily basis.

Over the years, Ian had picked up a few hobbies to fill in the time between shifts. He was an avid comic book collector, and he also liked to build model airplanes. One pastime that Ian had picked up in recent years was amateur photography. Five years ago, the fire department had hired a fire photographer named Ahmed. Ian and Ahmed shared many of the same shifts and had many long hours to get to know each other. Ahmed showed Ian many of his photos. Most of them were of fires or fire damage, but some of them were of other things, like Ahmed's family and the 1968 Camaro he had restored. Ahmed had won several awards for his bravery on the job and also for his stunning action photos, some of which had been featured in national publications.

Ahmed's love of photography eventually rubbed off on Ian, who decided to buy a camera. Ahmed gave Ian pointers while they were on duty at the station, and soon Ian became a bit of an expert himself. Ian's favorite subjects were his family, airplanes, and his dog, Blaze. Ian also learned a great deal about photographing fires and evidence from watching Ahmed.

After a few years, Ahmed received a job offer closer to where he grew up, in Miami. Both men were sad that they would no longer be working together, but they knew they could keep in touch and send each other their latest photographs via the Internet. Shortly after Ahmed left, the fire chief approached Ian to discuss a promotion.

"Ahmed said that he trained you to take over for him when he left. We don't have anyone else lined up, so if you want the job, it's yours."

At first, Ian thought about turning the job down. He was a firefighter, and he loved what he did. After giving it some thought, however, Ian realized that this was a great opportunity for him to continue working as a firefighter and to utilize his skills as a photographer in a professional capacity. He had never really thought about taking photographs professionally, but he was confident that with the training he had received from Ahmed, he could do the job. He decided to take the position of fire photographer.

Ian's schedule remained the same, but his pay went up. The city government began paying for his camera, supplies, and film. In addition, he was granted the opportunity to take a few photography classes at a local community college at the expense of the fire department, including darkroom techniques and forensics photography. What was once merely an enjoyable pastime for Ian had become the key to greater professional success. Photography was more than just a hobby for him now; it was a new and exciting way for him to keep fighting fires.

Other Professional Opportunities for Photographers

10

It is difficult to think of an area of modern life that is not affected by photography. Youth groups and churches often use photographers to help create newsletters. Cooks and chefs need photographers to create catalogs and cookbooks featuring shots of their finest creations. Web page designers usually use an abundance of photographs and other visual images to make their sites more attractive to browsers. And what would grandparents do without professional and amateur photographs of their precious grandchildren?

So far you have read about the photography professions that typically draw the greatest interest from practicing photographers. This last chapter is dedicated to additional photography professions that haven't been discussed in detail in this book. Although the information that follows is presented in relatively brief summaries, this is not to say that these photography careers are less important or attractive than the ones already mentioned. (To find additional information about these career options, refer to the For More Information section at the end of this book.)

Travel Photography

Professional travel photographers capture images of foreign locales for the purpose of revealing them to people who may not have the opportunity to see them, or for people who are thinking about taking a trip and would like a preview of what they are in for. Most travel photographers must be highly motivated and must like traveling constantly.

Travel photographers work for magazine publishers (primarily travel magazines), book publishers, trade publications, travel agencies and companies, cruise ships, museums, travel Web sites, newspapers, and stock houses. They can be full-time employees or they can work on a freelance basis. Sometimes employers will assign jobs to travel photographers, or sometimes travel photographers will pitch an assignment to their employers (not that they're always accepted). Some photographers who pursue this career make a name for themselves by writing the text that goes with the photos, whether for a tour guide, a magazine article, or a newspaper advertisement. Although you may end up paying for most or all of your supplies, many employers will pay for airfare, car rental, meals, hotels, and other expenses.

Requirements for this career may include a portfolio filled with forty or fifty photos of various fun-filled locations (most travel companies are primarily interested in areas of the world that are attractive to people looking for a relaxing vacation), strong communication skills, the ability to speak more than one language, strong technical skills, and, of course, a desire to travel. Travel photographers can make anywhere from $10 to $2,000 for a single photograph. The more experience you gain, the more you are likely to be paid.

Wildlife and Nature Photography

Much like travel photographers, wildlife and nature photographers capture images of flora, fauna, and landscapes that potential viewers may not otherwise get to see. They may also get to travel a great deal. Their photos are used for a wide range of purposes. Potential employers or buyers include book publishers, textbook manufacturers, calendar and greeting-card companies, magazine publishers, newspapers, government agencies, private organizations, Web sites, and stock houses. Both full-timers and freelancers can find work in this profession.

Many nature photographers consider themselves to be a cross between scientific photographers and artistic photographers. The images they capture commonly reveal a side of wildlife that many people simply never get to see. Although this career may seem perfect for the outdoors type and for adventurers (and to some extent it is), keep in mind that it also often entails a considerable amount of darkroom work, office time, and client meetings. Individuals interested in this type of photography should compile a portfolio dedicated to natural images while working on their technical skills. It may also help to concentrate on a single subject (for example, grizzly bears or mountainous terrain) in order to be able to present oneself as an expert in a specific area. This includes developing a heightened understanding of the subject itself, biologically, environmentally, and historically. It may also be a benefit to know more than one language, since you may need to travel to different countries to complete assignments. This is a difficult profession to break into, and you may need to develop it gradually as you work at another photography career. The pay scale is similar to that of travel photography.

Artistic Photography

Most photography experts agree that you need to have two things to succeed as an artistic photographer: creativity and luck. As with any art, it is nearly impossible to make a living as an artistic photographer. For every hundred photographs you submit to art journals or other publications, you may receive ninety-nine rejections—and a request to see more of your work with no promise that it will be accepted. However, all photographers need to have a strong sense of creativity, and it is comforting to know that while you may not make much money as an artistic photographer, you certainly will have plenty of career choices to fall back on.

Artistic photography is a career (or pastime) that requires a fresh vision of the world, a thorough knowledge of camera equipment and photography techniques, a strong appreciation for the work of other artists, "stick-to-itiveness," and enthusiasm. Sources that may be interested in your artistic photos include book publishers, magazine publishers, stock houses, galleries, museums, and private buyers. It is difficult to say how much you can make as an artistic photographer. On the one hand, you may make only $25 in a year by winning second place in a photography contest; on the other hand, you may become famous enough to sell your photos at whatever price you choose, even for thousands of dollars. When all is said and done, however, this thought remains at the heart of artistic photography: There is no universal reason to take artistic photos other than for the fact that it is something you enjoy doing. If you happen to make money as you do it, more power to you.

Photography Teacher

Teaching photography is a fulfilling career for those who have already experienced the world of professional photography and want to share their accumulated knowledge with others. As someone interested in photography and education, you have several roles to consider: high school teacher, college teacher, workshop instructor, or adult education instructor. Some experienced photographers mentor less experienced ones because they enjoy sharing and teaching the valuable knowledge they have amassed over their careers. One of these options may be perfect for you.

Individuals interested in teaching photography must have a love of photography, a desire to share that love with others, an understanding of teaching techniques, and a comprehensive knowledge of photography and its processes, equipment, techniques, applications, history, and masters. Some photographers teach full-time. Others teach part-time. Your salary will depend on where you teach, what type of institution you teach for, and your past experience with photography as well as with teaching. High schools generally pay photography teachers between $20,000 and $60,000 a year depending on experience; tenured college professors may make between $70,000 and $80,000 a year. Photographers who teach workshops and seminars may make somewhere between $100 and $3,000 per program. To become a full-time professional photography teacher at the high school level you will need to attain at least a master's degree; at the college level you may need a Ph.D.

Is That All?

No. That's not all. You can use your photography skills to excel at any number of related careers. The following is a list of a few of the more popular career choices.

Illustrator/Graphic Designer

- Illustrators create visual images for magazines, books, advertisements, posters, product packages, and other forms of visual media. Illustrators may use photographs, computer graphics, drawings, cartoons, and interesting fonts to make their work appealing to consumers. Graphic designers put these pieces together with text to create a visually pleasing product. Illustrators and graphic designers (who are often the same person) must be adept with a variety of computer programs, including photo-editing programs, word-processing programs, and illustration programs.

Photo Editor

- Since many newspapers and news magazines have large staffs of photographers, they also need photo editors or chief photographers.

Photo editors, although they might take a photograph or two themselves from time to time, are responsible for maintaining the scheduling and overall workload for staff photographers and freelance editors. As photo editor, you will work hand in hand with the editors and reporters to meet the visual needs of every article. A photo editor may also be expected to organize and maintain darkroom equipment and facilities, and to supervise all employees. Perhaps most important, a photo editor is expected to select the right photos for each article from an overabundance of shots of multiple events. The front-page shots are particularly vital: The photo editor is expected to use his or her photographic experience to quickly and efficiently create an overall look for the publication that is visually stimulating. Depending on the publication, this could happen on a monthly, weekly, or daily basis.

Videographer/Video Editor

• Videographers film events with video cameras and camcorders. Event photographers sometimes use video cameras and camcorders to record wedding ceremonies, graduations, sporting events, baptisms, and other events. Videographers may film events for insurance reasons. Models and actors may pay to have a film made of themselves to show future employers. Realtors may record videos of homes that are up for sale so that potential buyers can see them without visiting them. Video editors are adept at cutting and splicing videotape, matching sound with video, and otherwise creating flawless video presentations for professional purposes. Television companies and movie studios hire video editors to help produce a visually attractive product.

Gallery/Museum Director

• Art galleries and museums are run by professionals experienced in the production, sales, acquisition, and maintenance of artistic photographs and illustrations. Some photographic museums specialize in historic photographs and equipment. Others feature the work of our most talented artistic photographers, as well as up-and-coming photographers. Gallery directors may attain and inventory special types of photographs, for instance, Civil War photos. They may create a viable marketplace for those interested in buying artistic photographs. Gallery directors are most often self-employed and must work hard building a name for themselves.

Camera Buyer/Salesperson/Repair Person

• Those interested in the purchase, sales, and repair of cameras and camera equipment must stay on top of the industry by reading the latest product reviews, attending trade shows, and testing the equipment themselves. Buyers, salespersons, and repair persons may be able to get by with general photographic knowledge, although the more they know about photography the more successful they probably will be. These individuals will also need to have a sound understanding of sales techniques, as well as strong communication skills. Buyers who work for an employer must consistently be able to recommend beneficial products that meet financial parameters.

Photographic Writer

• A photographic writer is someone who writes about photography. It may seem obvious, but photographers make the best photographic writers. These individuals write camera reviews, photography advice columns, camera advertisements, and photography books. They write for trade magazines, travel magazines, newspapers, photography catalogs, and book publishers. Sometimes they are self-employed.

The Sky's the Limit!

The type of photography career that you eventually choose will depend on your personal interests. The bottom line is this: Get a camera, figure out how it works, and take photographs. No matter where your interests lie, there is certain to be a photography-related career for you somewhere; sometimes it takes a determined individual to create that career. The sky really is the limit within the world of photography professions.

Glossary

Many of the terms in the following list can be found in the text of this book. Some terms, however, do not appear in the text but were added to provide readers with a helpful guide for future reference. (For the definitions of basic camera parts, see the section titled Parts of a Camera in chapter 2.)

ambient light Consistent source of light surrounding the subject that isn't produced by the photographer. Daylight is considered ambient light.

audiovisual As the name implies, visual material such as filmstrips, films, and video combined with recorded sounds. This term is usually applied to demonstration techniques and classroom presentations. Sometimes called AV for short.

cable release Cable with a button on the end that can be used in place of the shutter release button. This piece of equipment is used to ensure that the camera does not move when taking a photograph.

camcorder Special video camera that also contains a videocassette recorder (VCR). A camcorder can record an event and play it back for future viewing. Camcorders can also be plugged into a television, and their tapes can be viewed on the television screen.

camera obscura Considered the earliest camera (first mentioned by Aristotle in the fourth century BC), the camera obscura is nothing more than a box with a pinhole in one side that projects an image of the outer world on the opposite wall of the box. Later versions of the camera obscura had light-sensitive paper inside them that captured the images cast through the pinholes.

close-up Photograph taken with the lens very close to the subject so it fills the frame of the finished photograph.

crop To print only part of a photo to achieve a more balanced, centered image. With digital photos, cropping can easily be accomplished with photo-editing software.

darkroom Light-free area needed to develop photographs without exposing them to light. A darkroom could be an old closet, a bathroom, a basement, or even a large bag in which the photographer can manipulate his or her materials. Some photographers use a developing tank, which is a light-free container designed to help process film.

definition The clarity of a photograph.

depth of field Term that refers to the area of the photograph that is in focus: the foreground, background, or both. Adjusting the aperture affects the depth of field.

developer Chemical used during the film developing process that causes the latent image to become visible on a negative or positive print. Developers actually cause silver particles in the film to turn black, thus becoming visible to the eye.

digital camera Camera that stores images as an electronic file, instead of on a roll of film. The images can then be moved from the camera's memory to a computer or CD for storage, or printed out on photographic paper.

double exposure Two photographs taken on a single frame of film.

electronic imaging Photographic technology that uses electronic currents to store photographic images, as used by VCRs and digital cameras.

emulsion The layers of light-sensitive chemicals suspended in gelatin that make up modern film.

enlarger Piece of equipment that produces prints by projecting a negative image onto light-sensitive paper.

existing light Natural light, or the light that is already existing before additional light is supplied for a shoot.

expose To allow light to hit film or photographic paper.

exposure Amount of light allowed to hit film inside a camera.

film Roll of flexible plastic coated with an emulsion used to capture images.

filter Colored piece of glass or plastic placed in front of the lens to change the color and appearance of a photograph.

fixed-focus Camera with a nonadjustable lens.

fixer Chemical used during the film developing
   process that prohibits light from further affecting
   a negative or positive print.

flash Lightbulb that supplies artificial light when
   a photograph is taken.

f-number Measurement of the size of the aperture on
   an adjustable camera.

focus To ensure that an image is clear and not hazy
   before taking a photograph.

frame Single picture on a roll of film.

f-stop Setting on an aperture ring that corresponds to
   an f-number.

hot shoe Part of a camera that holds a portable flash.

infrared light Light rays beyond the red end of the
   spectrum, thus invisible to the human eye.
   Special cameras can be used to capture
   infrared light.

latent image Invisible image left on film when it is
   exposed to light. This image is made visible
   during the developing process.

monopod Camera stand with one leg used to support
   the camera while taking a photograph.

negative Developed film. Negatives are so called
   because they display colors opposite of those that
   will make up the photograph.

overexposure Allowing too much light to hit the
   film. Overexposed film appears washed out
   and hazy.

panorama Photograph presenting an unbroken view
   of a landscape.

positive Finished photograph; sometimes called
   prints. Positives are made from negatives.

red eye When the flash reflects off the subject's retina. This causes the subject to seem to have red eyes in the final photograph.

safelight Special darkroom lamp used to prevent exposing film to damaging light.

simple camera Camera that does not need to be adjusted before taking a picture.

splice To remove a section of motion picture film and rejoin the loose ends. This process is also called film editing, and it is a common step in making motion pictures and television shows.

tabloid Newspaper of sensational material and format.

35 mm Very common type of film used in regular and motion picture cameras. This type of film is 35 millimeters wide.

toner Chemical that changes the color of a photographic print.

tripod Camera stand with three legs used to keep the camera steady.

underexposure Not allowing enough light to hit the film. Underexposed film appears dark and murky.

video Similar to motion pictures in that they both form a moving image to watch complete with sound, but video is actually quite different. Rather than recording actual photographs, video cameras and camcorders capture visual and audio stimulus as electrical currents, which are recorded on a videotape. When played back on a videocassette recorder (VCR), the electrical currents are transformed back into images and sounds on a television screen. Video "film" does not need to be developed like regular film.

For More Information

Publications

In the United States
American Cinematographer
1782 East 42nd Street
New York, NY 10017

American Photo
1633 Broadway
New York, NY 10017

Aperture
20 East 23rd Street
New York, NY 10010
Web site: http://www.aperture.org

Darkroom & Creative Camera Techniques
7800 Merrimac Avenue
Niles, IL 60714

Industrial Photography
PTN Publishing Company
445 Broad Hollow Road
Melville, NY 11747

Outdoor Photographer
12121 Wilshire Boulevard
Los Angeles, CA 90025
Web site: http://www.outdoorphotographer.com

Popular Photography
1633 Broadway
New York, NY 10019

Professional Photographer
229 Peachtree Street NE, Suite 2200
International Tower
Atlanta, GA 30303
Web site: http://www.ppmag.com

The Wedding Photographer
1312 Lincoln Boulevard
Santa Monica, CA 90406

In Canada
Photo Life
Apex Publications Inc.
One Dundas Street West, Suite 2500

P.O. Box 84
Toronto, ON M5G 1Z3
Web site: http://www.photolife.com

Professional Associations

In the United States

Advertising Photographers of New York
27 West 20th Street, Suite 601
New York, NY 10011
Web site: http://www.apany.com

American Photographic Artisan's Guild
P.O. Box 699
Fort Clinton, OH 43452

American Society of Media Photographers, Inc.
150 North Second Street
Philadelphia, PA 19106
Web site: http://www.asmp.org

American Society of Photographers
P.O. Box 3191
Spartanburg, SC 29304

American Society of Picture Professionals
409 South Washington Street
Alexandria, VA 22314
Web site: http://www.aspp.com

Associated Press
50 Rockefeller Plaza
New York, NY 10020
Web site: http://www.ap.org

Evidence Photographers International Council
600 Main Street
Honesdale, PA 18431
Web site: http://www.epic-photo.org

Friends of Photography
Ansel Adams Center
250 Fourth Street
San Francisco, CA 94103
Web site: http://www.friendsofphotography.org

The Imaging and Geospatial Information Society
5410 Grosvenor Lane, Suite 210
Bethesda, MD 20814-2160
Web site: http://www.asprs.org

International Association of Panoramic Photographers
P.O. Box 6550
Ellicot City, MD 21042
Web site: http://www.panphoto.com

International Center of Photography
1130 Fifth Avenue
New York, NY 10128
Web site: http://www.icp.org

International Freelance Photographers Organization
P.O. Box 777
Lewisville, NC 27023-0777
Web site: http://www.aipress.com

National Press Photographers Association, Inc.
3200 Croasdaile Drive, Suite 306
Durham, NC 27713
Web site: http://www.nppa.org

North American Nature Photography Association
10200 West Forty-fourth Avenue
Wheat Ridge, CO 80033-2840
Web site: http://www.nanpa.org

Photographic Society of America
3000 United Founders Boulevard, Suite 103
Oklahoma City, OK 73112-3940
Web site: http://www.psa-photo.org

Photo Traveler: Travel Guides for Photographers
P.O. Box 39912
Los Angeles, CA 90039
Web site: http://phototravel.com

Picture Agency Council of America (PACA)
P.O. Box 308
Northfield, MN 55057-0308
Web site: http://www.pacaoffice.org

Professional Photographers of America, Inc.
229 Peachtree Street NE, Suite 2200

Atlanta, GA 30303
Web site: http://www.ppa.com

The Society for Imaging Science and Technology
7003 Kilworth Lane
Springfield, VA 22151
Web site: http://www.imaging.org

Society of American Travel Writers
1500 Sunday Drive, Suite 102
Raleigh, NC 27607
Web site: http://www.satw.org

Technical Association for the Graphic Arts
68 Lomb Memorial Drive
Rochester, NY 14623-5604
Web site: http://www.taga.org

Wedding Photographers International
P.O. Box 1703
Santa Monica, CA 90406

White House News Photographers Association
7119 Ben Franklin Station
Washington, DC 20044-7119
Web site: http://www.whnpa.org

In Canada

Canadian Association for Photographic Art
3158 Hopedale Avenue
Clearbrook, BC V2T 2G7
Web site: http://www.capa-acap.ca

Canadian Association of Journalists
St. Patrick's Building
Carleton University
1125 Colonel By Drive
Ottawa, ON K1S 5B6
Web site: http://www.eagle.ca/caj

Canadian Association of Photographers and Illustrators
  in Communications
100 Broadview Avenue, Suite 322
Toronto, ON M4M 3H3
Web site: http://www.capic.org

The Professional Photographers of Canada
1215 Penticton Avenue
Penticton, BC V2A 2N3
Web site: http://www.ppoc.ca

Professional Photographers of Ontario
2833 Donnelly Drive, RR #4
Kemptville, ON K0G 1J0
Web site: http://www.professionalphotographers
  ofontario.com

Colleges/Universities with Photography Programs

In the United States
Amarillo College Photography
P.O. Box 447

Amarillo, TX 79178-0001
Web site: http://www.actx.edu/~photography

Arizona State University
University Drive and Mill Avenue
Tempe, AZ 85287
Web site: http://www.asu.edu

Brooks Institute of Photography
801 Alston Road
Santa Barbara, CA 93108
http://www.brooks.edu

California State University, Fullerton
P.O. Box 34080
Fullerton, CA 92834
Web site: http://www.fullerton.edu

Colorado Mountain College (Central Administration and
    Admissions Office)
831 Grand Avenue
P.O. Box 10001
Glenwood Springs, CO 81602
Web site: http://www.coloradomtn.edu/programs/php

Maine College of Art
97 Spring Street
Portland, ME 04101
http://www.meca.edu

New England School of Photography
537 Commonwealth Avenue

Boston, MA 02215
Web site: http://www.nesop.com

Oklahoma School of Photography
2306 North Moore Avenue
Moore, OK 73160
Web site: http://www.photocareers.com/index.html

Oregon College of Art & Craft
8245 SW Barnes Road
Portland, OR 97225
Web site: http://www.ocac.edu

School of Visual Arts
209 East 23rd Street
New York, NY 10010-3994
http://www.schoolofvisualarts.edu/sva.html

In Canada
Alberta College of Art and Design
1407 Fourteenth Avenue NW
Calgary, AB T2N 4R3
Web site: http://www.acad.ab.ca

Dawson Institute of Photography (Centre for Imaging
    Arts & Information Technologies)
4001 de Maisonneuve West
Suite 2G.2
Montréal, PQ H3Z 3G4

Nova Scotia College of Art and Design (NASCAD)
5163 Duke Street
Halifax, NS B3J 3J6
Web site: http://www.nscad.ns.ca

Web Sites/E-Zines

The following Web sites offer a wide range of resources for photographers, including museums, tutorials, job listings, workshop and contest information, where to find equipment and supplies, and other resources.

Apogee Photo
http://www.apogeephoto.com/home.html

Center for Creative Photography at the University
  of Arizona
http://dizzy.library.arizona.edu/branches/ccp/
ccphome.html

Darkroom Source
http://darkroomsource.com/accessories.htm

Digital Camera Resource Page
http://www.dcresource.com

George Eastman House, International Museum of
  Photography and Film
http://www.eastman.org

Government Jobs
http://www.govjob.com/index.htm

Nature Photographers
http://www.naturephotographers.net

New York Institute of Photography
http://www.nyip.com

Photographer's Associations
http://www.generation.net/~gjones/assoc.htm

The Photographic Historical Society
http://www.rit.edu/~andpph/tphs.html

Photography Clubs and Organizations
http://space.tin.it/arte/wvgal/photoclubs.html

Photo Magazine:The Online Photo Magazine
http://www.photomagazine.com

Photo.net
http://www.photo.net

Photoquest
http://www.photoquest.com

Photo Resource Magazine
http://www.photoresource.com

Studio Photography & Design
http://www.spdonline.com

Underwater Photo Internet Ring
http://diveflag.com/uwphotoring

U.S. Office of Personnel
http://www.usajobs.opm.gov/index.htm

For Further Reading

Arndt, David. *How to Shoot and Sell Sports Photography*. Buffalo, NY: Amherst Media, 1999.

Boursier, Helen T. *Family Portrait Photography: Professional Techniques and Images*. Buffalo, NY: Amherst Media, 1999.

Box, Douglas Allen. *Professional Secrets of Wedding Photography*. Buffalo, NY: Amherst Media, 2000.

Braun, Brad. *Learn Digital Photography in a Weekend*. Rocklin, CA: Prima Tech, 1998.

Cantrell, Bambi, and Skip Cohen. *The Art of Wedding Photography: Professional Techniques with Style*. New York: Amphoto Books, 2000.

Cohen, Stuart. *Photographer's Resource: The Watson-Guptill Guide to Workshops, Conferences, Artists'*

Colonies, Academic Programs, Digital Imaging Programs, On-the-Road Programs. New York: Watson-Guptill, 1997.

Demaio, Joe, Robin Worth, and Dennis Curtin. *The New Darkroom Handbook: A Complete Guide to the Best Design, Construction, and Equipment.* Boston: Focal Press, 1998.

Eggers, Ron. *Basic Digital Photography.* Buffalo, NY: Amherst Media, 2000.

Engh, Rohn. *Sell & Re-Sell Your Photos.* Cincinnati, OH: Writer's Digest Books, 1997.

Engh, Rohn. *SellPhotos.com.* Cincinnati, OH: Writer's Digest Books, 2000.

Horton, Brian. *Associated Press Guide to Photojournalism.* New York: McGraw-Hill, 2000.

Johnson, Bervin M. *Opportunities in Photography Careers.* Lincolnwood, IL: VGM Career Horizons, 1999.

King, Julie Adair. *Digital Photography for Dummies.* Indianapolis, IN: IDG Books Worldwide, 1998.

Krejcarek, Philip. *Digital Photography: A Hands-On Introduction.* Albany, NY: Delmar Publishers, 1997.

Langford, Michael. *Basic Photography.* Boston: Focal Press, 1997.

Monteith, Ann. *The Business of Wedding Photography.* New York: Watson-Guptill, 1996.

Schaefer, John. *The Ansel Adams Guide: Basic Techniques of Photography.* Boston: Little, Brown & Company, 1999.

Shaw, John. *John Shaw's Nature Photography Field Guide:* Rev. ed. New York: Amphoto Books, 2000.

Siljander, Raymond P., and Darin D. Fredrickson. *Applied Police & Fire Photography.* Springfield, IL: Charles C. Thomas Publisher, 1997.

117

Tarrant, Jon. *Professional Press, Editorial and PR Photography.* Boston: Focal Press, 1998.

Wildi, Ernst. *Achieving the Ultimate Image.* Buffalo, NY: Amherst Media, 1998.

Willins, Michael. *The Photographer's Market Guide to Photo Submission and Portfolio Formats.* Cincinnati, OH: Writer's Digest Books, 1997.

Yate, Martin J. *Resumes That Knock 'Em Dead.* Holbrook, MA: Adams Media Corporation, 2001.

Index

About the Author

Greg Roza writes and edits for a children's book publisher located in western New York. In his spare time he teaches poetry at SUNY Fredonia and edits a humor Web site. Greg has a wife named Abigail and a two-year-old daughter named Autumn.